lonely planet

POCKET ORLANDO & Walt Disney World® Resort

Amy Bizzari & Sarah Etinas

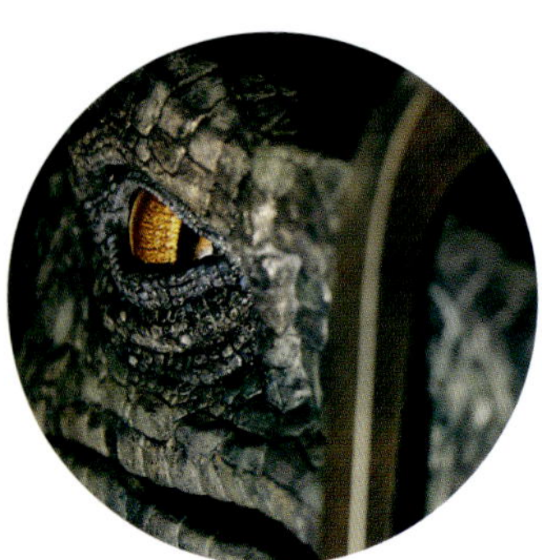

Top: Jurassic World VelociCoaster (p105)
Bottom: Goofy and Cinderella Castle, The Magic Kingdom (p39)

Contents

FROM TOP LEFT: UNIVERSAL ORLANDO ©, DISNEY ©

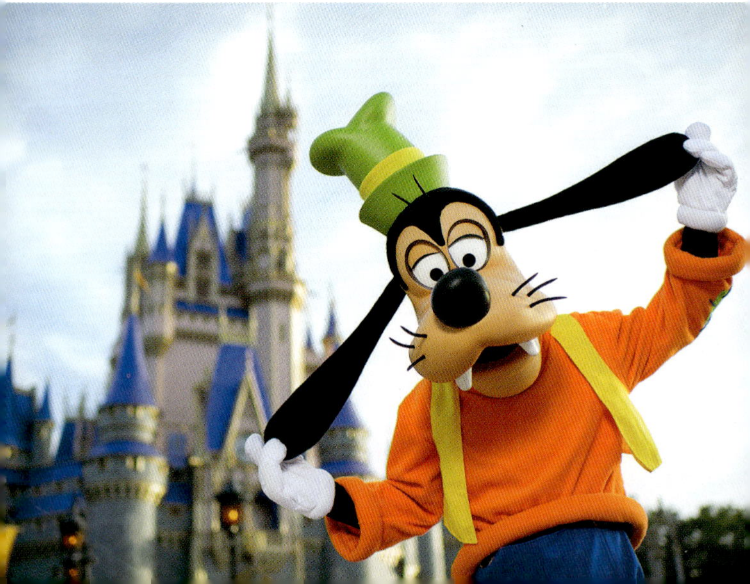

Explore Walt Disney World® Resort 31

Explore Universal Orlando Resort 87

Explore Orlando & Beyond 116

★ Worth A Trip

Toolkit 145

★ Top Experiences

The Journey Begins Here

Walt Disney World holds so many memories for me, beginning with my first visit with my parents and sister, when I still believed that the characters strolling the Magic Kingdom were real. Today, I happily share the magic with my own children, who love nothing more than to see their mom laugh with joy while swirling on the teacups at the Mad Tea Party or scream her head off while zooming down Space Mountain. My kids are no longer littles, but Walt Disney World continues to bring us together, creating new moments to cherish each time we visit.

Amy Bizzarri
@amybizzarri

Amy is a Chicago-based travel writer. When she's not having fun in Tomorrowland, you can find her riding her bike along Lake Michigan or strolling her North Side neighborhood, Lincoln Square.

Sarah Etinas
sarahetinas.com

Sarah is a freelance travel writer and editor. Find her exploring the world one sunny beach and innovative restaurant at a time.

Toy Story Land, Disney's Hollywood Studios (p56)

TOY
STORY
LAND

THE BEST

Character Meet-and-Greets

Character meals and interactive shows are just some of the ways to get face-to-face with favorite characters like Mickey, Minnie, Shrek, Elsa and Scooby Doo. These experiences are popular so plan ahead.

Meet Cinderella, Tiana and a rotating lineup of other princesses at **Fairytale Hall**. (Magic Kingdom; p45)

Find classic characters like Mickey, Minnie, Snow White and Tinker Bell at the **Town Square Theater**. (Magic Kingdom; pictured above; p46)

Hang out with Goofy, Minnie and Donald in their circus performer outfits under the big tent at **Storybook Circus**. (Magic Kingdom; p47)

Meet one of your heroes – from Storm and Spidey to Wolverine – at the **Marvel Character Dinner**. (Islands of Adventure; pictured above; p108)

Head to **Chef Mickey's** to share a meal with Donald, Goofy and friends. (Disney Contemporary Resort; p85)

Dine in the castle with Cinderella herself at **Cinderella's Royal Table**. (Magic Kingdom; p48)

Right: Fantasmic!, Disney's Hollywood Studios (p55)

THE BEST

Roller Coasters

Orlando is home to some of the most exhilarating roller coasters in the world, where adrenaline junkies can experience heart-pounding drops, twists and turns.

Rocket through the dark on **Space Mountain**, Disney's classic coaster that careens through star-filled galaxies. (Magic Kingdom; p42)

Sway through Snow White's story on the **Seven Dwarfs Mine Train**, where sparkling gems and seven quirky miners await. (for under 10s; Magic Kingdom; p41)

Soar over London and Neverland on **Peter Pan's Flight**, a good option for younger kids and a gentle journey through the classic tale. (for under 10s; Magic Kingdom; p41)

The **Revenge of the Mummy** twists through the catacombs in near total darkness. (Universal Studios; pictured above left; p98)

Journey to the heart of Harry Potter's Forbidden Forest on **Hagrid's Magical Creatures Motorbike Adventure**. (Islands of Adventure; pictured above; p103)

Race through a dinosaur-infested jungle at 70mph on Universal Studios' biggest, baddest scream machine, the **Jurassic World VelociCoaster**. (Islands of Adventure; p105)

Right: Jurassic World VelociCoaster (p105)

THE BEST

Splashdowns

Dive into the ultimate aquatic adventure and get your splash on at Orlando's best water parks, where thrilling slides, lazy rivers and wave pools promise a refreshing escape from the Florida heat.

Plummet down a near-vertical drop at high speeds aboard **Summit Plummet**, one of the most thrilling water rides in Orlando. (Blizzard Beach; p82)

Slide through an abandoned fruit-processing plant before a final plunge into Hideaway Bay on the **Crush 'n' Gusher**. (Typhoon Lagoon; p82)

Ride through a giant half-pipe where rafts spin and plunge at **Orange Rush**. (Legoland Water Park; p142)

Set off on a high-speed water adventure on the **Krakatau Aqua Coaster**, which takes your canoe on a toboggan-style track past a towering volcano. (Volcano Bay; p112)

Join Tiana on a paddle through the bayou on **Tiana's Bayou Adventure**, where you'll experience exciting twists, turns and splashes as you navigate the Louisiana swamp. (Magic Kingdom; p43)

Krakatau Aqua Coaster, Volcano Bay (p112)

THE BEST

Fantasy Lands

Orlando's immersive attractions, also known as dark rides, transport you to fantastical worlds with captivating stories, stunning visuals and interactive 4D experiences that ignite the imagination.

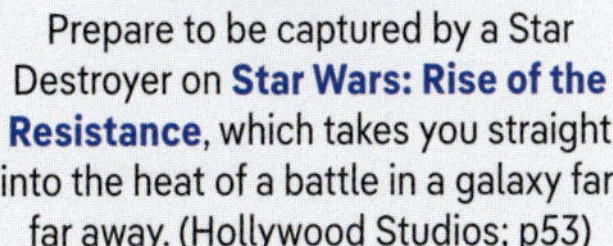

Prepare to be captured by a Star Destroyer on **Star Wars: Rise of the Resistance**, which takes you straight into the heat of a battle in a galaxy far, far away. (Hollywood Studios; p53)

Check into the 'hotel' inspired by the classic mid-century TV series, but beware of the jaw-dropping elevator on the **Twilight Zone Tower of Terror**. (Hollywood Studios; pictured above; p54)

Brave the white-knuckle 3D roller coaster **Harry Potter and the Escape from Gringotts** as you try to break out of the goblins' bank with Harry, Ron and Hermione. (Universal Studios; pictured above; p97)

Fly around the Earth aboard the flight simulator **Soarin' Around the World**, where riders are seated in a hang-glider-like row that lifts into a dome screen. (Epcot; p63)

Universal Studios Store, Universal CityWalk (p110)

THE BEST

Shopping Experiences

Orlando is a shopper's paradise that extends well beyond the iconic Mickey Mouse ears, with a diverse array of unique boutiques, trendy outlets and luxurious malls that cater to every style and budget.

Drop by **World of Disney**, the world's largest Disney store, which offers an incredible selection of merchandise for all ages. (Disney Springs; p85)

Sift through the racks at the **Emporium** on Main Street, USA, a classic Disney shop with a wide variety of souvenirs, apparel and collectibles. (Magic Kingdom; p49)

Bust out the credit card for the **Universal Studios Store** for collectibles from Universal movies. (Universal CityWalk; p110)

Get ready for a permanent vacation at the Smuggler's Hold in **Jimmy Buffet's Margaritaville**, which spills over with island-style decor. (Universal CityWalk; p110)

Step into **Memento Mori**, where you'll find a selection of spooky souvenirs, eerie collectibles and exclusive Haunted Mansion-themed merchandise. (Magic Kingdom; p49)

THE BEST

Golf Courses

Walt Disney World® is a golfer's paradise with world-class courses created by renowned designers, where you can experience the magic of Disney while enjoying a round on pristine greens.

Challenge yourself at **Disney's Magnolia Golf Course**, set amid the natural beauty of Florida woodlands and a favorite with serious golfers.

Admire the stunning design of **Disney's Palm Golf Course** with its shimmering lakes and tropical sands – this course is both a beauty and a fun challenge.

Test your approach shot at the classic country-club style course, **Disney's Lake Buena Vista Golf Course**, perfect for those looking for a traditional golfing experience with a touch of Disney magic.

Enjoy a quick round of golf at **Disney's Oak Trail Golf Course**, a scenic, relaxing nine-hole walking course.

Enjoy a whimsical mini-golf experience with Disney characters and themes at **Winter Summerland Miniature Golf**, perfect for the whole family.

FROM MR.SOMCHAI SUKKASEM/SHUTTERSTOCK ©, TAWAN75/SHUTTERSTOCK ©

THE BEST

Cultural Experiences

Thought Orlando was just theme parks? Think again.

Admire exhibits at the **Wells' Built Museum** in downtown Orlando, which include artifacts from the local Civil Rights movement and memorabilia from famous African American performers. (p134)

Have lunch with an astronaut at the **Kennedy Space Center**, an out-of-this-world dining experience where you get to hear firsthand stories from a real astronaut about historic space missions. (p138)

Learn about Walt Disney's life, achievements and the history of the parks at **Walt Disney Presents**, home to a number of rare artifacts. (p54)

Journey to outer space with a 180-degree immersive view via the **Orlando Science Center's** mega screen CineDome. (p135)

Admire the landscapes of the Florida Highwaymen at the **Orlando Museum of Art**. (p135)

Kennedy Space Center (p138)

Best for Kids Under 10

Take toddlers to the miniature Alpine village of **Fantasyland**, filled with storybook rides and princesses galore. (Magic Kingdom; p41)

Embark on a Disney-style trip to the zoo, with animal habitats and a safari expedition. Interactive exhibits, like **Rafiki's Planet Watch**, offer educational fun. (Animal Kingdom; p76)

Travel the globe at the **World Showcase**, where kids can meet characters in their countries of origin, like Elsa in Norway or Mulan in China. (Epcot; p61)

Eat green eggs and ham at **Seuss Landing**, a whimsical, colorful world where Dr Seuss' beloved characters and stories come to life. (Islands of Adventure; p107)

Enjoy the smaller scale and gentle rides of **Legoland**, a less-crowded alternative to the mainstay theme parks. (p142)

Best for Free

Stroll Disney's free **BoardWalk**, near Epcot, for a lively waterfront experience complete with street performers and live music. (p82)

Enjoy live music and entertainment at the Waterside Stage and Marketplace Stage in **Disney Springs**, while the kids have a blast at the splash pads located near the Marketplace. (p79)

Watch street performances and window-shop at **CityWalk** at Universal Studios Orlando, a free 30-acre entertainment complex, which also has fountains for kids to play in. (p110)

Shop for fresh produce and people-watch at the **Orlando Farmers Market**, held on Sundays at Lake Eola Park. It's one of the best spots in town for an impromptu picnic. (p134)

Sample wine at the **Lakeridge Winery & Vineyards**, Florida's largest vineyard, which hosts free tastings and tours of the estate. (p124)

Perfect Days

Discover the ultimate guide to Orlando. From one-day highlights and extended-stay tips to rainy-day adventures, we have the perfect itinerary for every scenario at Disney World and beyond.

Germany Pavilion, World Showcase (p62)

ALL IMAGES: DISNEY ©

DAY ONE

Only Have One Day?

MORNING

Make a beeline to the **Magic Kingdom** (p39) for the rope drop, which ushers in the day's first guests. Hop on all the classic rides, from **Dumbo the Flying Elephant** (p47; pictured) to **Alice's Mad Tea Party** (p41). Enjoy lunch with the Beast at **Be Our Guest Restaurant** (p48).

AFTERNOON

Head to Adventureland and Tomorrowland, visiting attractions like the **Jungle Cruise** (p43) and **Space Mountain** (p42). Cool off with a refreshing Dole Whip ice cream at **Aloha Isle** (p49).

EVENING

Enjoy the enchanting **fireworks display** (p44) over Cinderella Castle, a perfect end to a magical day. Head to **Main Street, USA** (p45), for souvenir shopping and a final look at the illuminated park before heading home.

DAY TWO

A Weekend Trip

MORNING

On your second day, head to **Epcot** (p59) and journey across the Earth on **Soarin' Around the World** (p63), where you feel like you're flying over iconic landmarks.

AFTERNOON

Design and test your own high-speed car at **Test Track** (p63), set sail on a boat ride through innovative farming on **Living with the Land** (p64) and explore the ocean at the **Seas with Nemo & Friends** (p65).

EVENING

Travel the globe at the **World Showcase** (p61; pictured) and dine at one of the many country pavilions, including China, Italy and Mexico.

DAY THREE

A Short Break

MORNING

Head to **Hollywood Studios** (p51) and kick off your day with the exhilarating **Star Wars: Rise of the Resistance** (p53), an immersive journey into the Star Wars universe. Cool off with a glass of otherworldly Blue Milk at the **Milk Stand** (p57).

AFTERNOON

Plunge into the thrilling world of the **Twilight Zone Tower of Terror** (p54; pictured), where you'll experience a heart-in-your-throat free-fall. Refuel with a Mickey Brownie Sundae at **Hollywood Scoops** (p56).

EVENING

Enjoy a classic martini at the **Hollywood Brown Derby** (p57), a replica of the original. Wrap up your adventure by catching the stunning **Fantasmic!** (p55) nighttime show, complete with fireworks and water effects.

If You Have More Time

Go early to **Universal Studios** (p93) and make a beeline for the **Wizarding World of Harry Potter: Diagon Alley**; guests of Universal Orlando resort hotels can get into Harry Potter attractions one hour before everyone else.

Scream with delight as you dodge Bellatrix Lestrange on **Harry Potter & the Escape from Gringotts**, then hop on the **Hogwarts Express** to **Hogsmeade** at the Islands of Adventure park (p101, multipark pass required).

Ride **Hagrid's Magical Creatures Motorbike Adventure** before refueling with butterbeer at the **Three Broomsticks**. Digested your meal? Good, because now it's time to pick your coaster – the **Incredible Hulk Coaster**, which packs the g-force of a fighter jet or, if you've got the nerve, the terrifying **Jurassic World VelociCoaster**, which includes a zero-gravity 100ft inverted stall. Gulp...

After another Marvel superhero ride or two, head back to **CityWalk** (p110) and relax over a unique burger-sushi combo at the ever-popular **Cowfish**.

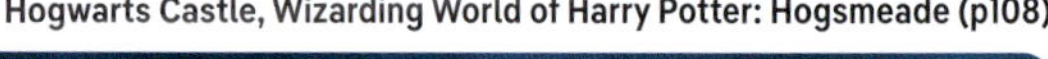

Hogwarts Castle, Wizarding World of Harry Potter: Hogsmeade (p108)

A City Day Trip

Spending a day in Orlando without visiting the theme parks can be a delightful experience. Start your morning with a visit to **Lake Eola Park** (p135), where you can enjoy a leisurely paddle around the lake.

For a more cultural outing, check out the latest exhibit at the **Orlando Museum of Art** (p135). At lunch, try **Little Saigon** (p136) for a bowl of pho.

In the afternoon, explore the boutiques and farmers market of **Winter Park** (pictured; p124).

End your day with a visit to Icon Park for a ride on the 400ft **Orlando Eye** (p122), which has soaring views of the city.

On a Rainy Day

There are plenty of indoor activities to keep the entire family entertained when it rains. Visit the **Orlando Science Center** (p135) for hands-on exhibits and interactive displays.

Another favorite is **Dezerland Park Orlando** (p122), which has everything from indoor bumper cars to go-karts.

Spend time at **Crayola Experience** (p125), where kids can unleash their creativity with various arts and crafts activities.

Enjoy a movie at one of the AMC Theatres in **Disney Springs** or go bowling or play billiards at **Splitsville Luxury Lane** (pictured).

End the day with giant ice cream sundaes in **Disney Springs** (p79).

Get Prepared

BOOK AHEAD

For **Walt Disney World®**, it's best to book your park tickets as early as possible, ideally six months to a year in advance, especially if you're visiting during peak seasons like summer or holidays.

For **Universal Orlando**, booking tickets at least a month or two in advance is recommended to take advantage of discounts and ensure availability during busy times.

Manners Matter

When visiting theme parks in Orlando, remember that tipping is standard. Tip all service staff, including servers, bellhops and housekeeping. If you're visiting from abroad, know that personal space is valued – Americans generally prefer to keep a comfortable distance from others, even in crowded places. Lastly, queue etiquette is important; cutting in line is considered rude, and it's expected that everyone should wait their turn patiently.

Wait Times

Wait times at the theme parks can be looong. Popular rides like Space Mountain, for example, can have wait times of 40 minutes or more. Use the theme park apps to check real-time wait times and make sure to plan your day around less crowded attractions. For the shortest lines, arrive early or stay late. Use Lightning Lane or Universal Express passes (p157) to skip to the front of the line.

Things to Know

Arrive at the park at least 30 minutes before gates open. Don't window-shop or dawdle – just march straight to the rides.

Create a flexible itinerary that prioritizes must-see attractions and includes downtime to avoid burnout.

Stay at a resort hotel. While it's tempting to save money by staying elsewhere, the value of staying at the resort lies in the convenience – including early entry. These hotels are divided into value, midrange and deluxe categories.

Utilize park apps to check ride wait times and make dining reservations in advance.

Pack essentials like sunscreen, refillable water bottles and comfortable shoes to stay hydrated and comfortable throughout your visit.

Keyless storage lockers are located near park entrances, and cost $10 to $15 for the day.

TIPPING

In Orlando, and the greater US, tipping is a customary practice to show appreciation for good service and it significantly contributes to the income of service workers. Carrying small bills will make tipping easier and more convenient.

Restaurants
of the bill

Bellhops & housekeeping
per bag or day

Taxis & rideshares
of the fare

Shuttle drivers
per bag

DAILY BUDGET

BUDGET: Less than $300

- Value resort room for four: **$200**
- Self-catering and cheap eats: **$40-60**
- Seven-day bus pass: **$16**

MIDRANGE: $400-500

- Theme-park accommodations for four: **$300**
- Multiday theme-park ticket: **$50-120**
- Car rental per week: **$300-400**

TOP END: More than $500

- Luxury theme-park accommodations for four: from **$400**
- Theater ticket: **$40-80**
- Themed Disney dining or top-end restaurant: **$100-200**

Currency
US dollar ($)

Language
English

Time zone
Eastern Standard Time (GMT/UTC minus five hours)

TOMAS RAGINA/SHUTTERSTOCK ©

TIP

Planning your visit during the shoulder season means smaller crowds, milder weather, cheaper lodging and a more relaxed experience. The best months are September through February and May. Spring break and summer vacation will be busy.

When To Go

There are only two seasons in Orlando: summer and winter. Summer starts in May and extends into September; winter lasts from October through April.

March to May is a great time to visit, though because of spring break you should expect peak crowds. Summer is hot, humid and busy with families on vacation and events like GayDays (June) and Independence Day (July). Hurricane season runs from June to November, though the crowds thin out as kids return to school. Tourism spikes again at Thanksgiving, which kicks off the start of the holiday season. Christmas festivities continue throughout the month of December.

The Big Events

Usually held February & March: Parades, live music and Cajun food mimic New Orleans' iconic street festival, **Mardi Gras**. The crowds really get into the whole spirit of catching beads and the floats are beautifully decorated.

October: Dress in your favorite costumes and enjoy special Halloween-themed parades and character meet-and-greets at **Mickey's Not-So-Spooky Halloween Party**. Trick-or-treat stations are scattered throughout the Magic Kingdom.

September & October: Halloween Horror Nights sees 10 warehouses converted into scary mazes themed according to either a well-known horror franchise or Universal's own dastardly creations. The frights are very real – it's not for children 13 and under.

Early November–Christmas: The official holiday celebration at Disney is **Mickey's Very Merry Christmas Party**, held on select nights at the Magic Kingdom. The festivities transform the park into a winter wonderland with parades.

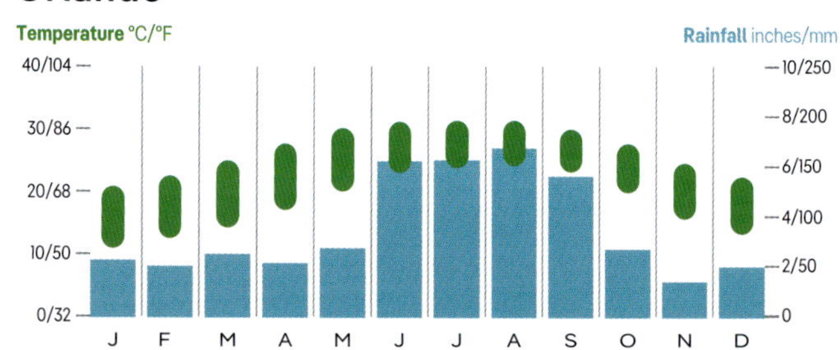

Mardi Gras

Artsy & Interesting

Late March–July: At the **Epcot International Flower & Garden Festival** you can admire stunning topiary displays of your favorite Disney characters from around the world and enjoy live music.

April: The week-long **Florida Film Festival** features a wide selection of independent films, documentaries and shorts. It's a must-visit for film enthusiasts.

May: The **Orlando International Fringe Theater Festival** (p98) celebrates the performing arts with a diverse range of theater, comedy, music and dance performances. It's a vibrant showcase of talent from artists around the world.

June: The massive five-day celebration known as **GayDays Orlando** is one of several LGBTIQ+ events held in early summer. Theme park days take place at Walt Disney World®, Universal Orlando and SeaWorld.

ACCOMMODATIONS LOWDOWN

Orlando accommodations range from budget-friendly hotels to luxury resorts. Prices peak during holidays and school vacations, while off-season months like September offer better deals. Travelers can find bargains by booking early, using discount sites or considering accommodations slightly outside major attractions for lower rates.

Getting There

Orlando International Airport (MCO) offers numerous amenities, daily nonstop international flights and good transportation options, including taxis, rideshares and shuttles to Universal (10 miles) and Disney World (25 miles).

From the MCO Airport to the Theme Parks

Rideshare

The best way to get from the airport to Walt Disney World® or Universal Studios is via a rideshare service like Uber or Lyft. Trips to resorts typically take about 30 minutes and cost on average $35 to $50.

Shuttle Services

Shuttle services from the airport to the resorts include options like **Mears Connect** (*round-trip adult/child $32/26*). Many hotels near the I-4 offer inexpensive shuttles to area theme parks. If you're staying in a hotel on **International Drive**, consider purchasing an I-Ride Trolley day pass (*$6*), which stops at six smaller theme parks.

Rental Car

Renting a car in Orlando gives you flexibility and freedom, but if you're just visiting the theme parks, you'll find there are more efficient transportation and cheaper options like shuttles, rideshares and buses.

Bus

Orlando's bus service, Lynx (*single fare $2*), offers extensive routes throughout the city and surrounding areas. At the airport you can catch buses like line 11, which connects the airport to downtown Orlando (*45 minutes*), and line 42, which goes to International Drive (*one hour*).

Other Points of Entry

The **Brightline train** offers a high-speed, comfortable travel experience between Miami and Orlando (*from $110, 3½ hours*), with stops in Aventura, Fort Lauderdale, Boca Raton and West Palm Beach. Purchase tickets online, arrive at the station early and enjoy amenities like Wi-Fi and snacks during your journey.

Amtrak's **Silver Meteor** runs from New York City to Miami with stops in over two dozen cities, including Philadelphia, Washington (DC), Richmond, Raleigh, Charleston, Savannah and Orlando. Tickets from New York cost from $160/1050 (*coach/private room*); the journey takes around 24 hours.

Getting Around

Disney is vast. Its transportation system utilizes boats, buses and even a monorail to shuttle visitors to hotels, theme parks and other attractions within the resort's 47 sq miles. The Universal parks are also linked by walkways, boats and shuttles. It's a short walk or boat ride from most Universal resort hotels to the theme parks.

Disney Resorts

Transportation & Ticket Center

Parking lots sit directly outside the gates of all the parks, except for the Magic Kingdom. If you're driving to the latter, you'll need to park at the **Transportation & Ticket Center** (*TTC; parking from $30 per day*), Disney's transportation epicenter. If you are driving to the Magic Kingdom, you will park here. If you are staying at a Disney resort, you may also pass through this hub on your way to one of the other parks. Boats, shuttles and the monorail all depart from the TTC.

With its massive parking lot and endless lines for bus shuttles, the TTC can be frustrating way to start to your Disney day. Magic Kingdom park-goers should consider taking a cab to a Magic Kingdom resort and then hopping on the monorail or boat to the theme park instead. Another strategy is to reserve a breakfast or dinner at one of these resorts (many offer character meals), as restaurant reservations allow you to park at the resort free of charge.

ESSENTIAL APP

Download the **My Disney Experience** app or the **Universal Orlando Resort** app before your trip.

When planning, remember that it can take an hour to get from point A to point B using the Disney transportation system, and there is not always a direct route.

Note: it's not made clear, but parking tickets bought at one park are good all day for all Disney parks.

Monorail & Disney Skyliner

The Walt Disney World Monorail has three free lines for guests. The **Resort Monorail Line** serves the TTC, the Magic Kingdom Park, Disney's Polynesian Village Resort, Disney's Grand Floridian Resort & Spa, and Disney's Contemporary Resort. The **Magic Kingdom Express Line** is the same route, but only stops at the Magic Kingdom and the TTC. The **Epcot Line** runs between Epcot and the TTC.

The **Disney Skyliner** is a nifty 60ft-high gondola that connects Hollywood Studios and Epcot with four resort hotels.

Bus

Everything at Disney World is accessible via free buses, charmingly wrapped with Disney characters, but not all destinations are directly connected. Buses from Disney Springs, for example, do not connect directly to any theme parks. To this end, some routes may involve a combination of bus, monorail or boat. Use the My Disney Experience app to check schedules and plan routes.

Boat

Disney World Water Transportation runs complimentary Disney boats – from water taxis to 600-passenger ferries – that connect Disney resorts to different theme parks and the TTC. Boats also loop between Epcot, Hollywood Studios, BoardWalk, Disney's Yacht & Beach Club Resorts and Walt Disney World Swan & Dolphin Resorts. Use the My Disney Experience app to check schedules and plan routes.

Minnie Vans

For quick, point-to-point drop-offs and pickups around Walt Disney World, take a polka-dotted Minnie Van. Download the Lyft app and select a Minnie Van vehicle to pick you up. Guests can also use Lyft to request an accessible Minnie Van. All Minnie Vans come equipped with two complimentary seats for tiny travelers.

From Orlando

Orlando's Lynx bus 50 connects the downtown central station to Disney's Transportation & Ticket Center and Disney Springs, but it's an hour ride.

Universal Studios

Universal Orlando Resort – including the resort hotels, Islands of Adventure, Universal Studios, Universal Epic Universe and CityWalk – are all linked by pedestrian walkways. It's a 10- to 15-minute walk from the theme parks and CityWalk to the deluxe resort hotels.

Boat

Water taxis, which leave roughly every 15 minutes, shuttle between four of the Universal hotels and CityWalk. From here, it's a five-minute walk across the canal to the theme parks.

Hogwarts Express

Undoubtedly the coolest way to get around is aboard the Hogwarts Express, which runs between the 9¾ platform at King's Cross Station (Universal Studios) and Hogsmeade (Islands of Adventure). You'll need a park-to-park ticket to take the train.

Parking

Parking for Universal Studios, Islands of Adventure, Universal Epic Universe and CityWalk is available inside a giant garage structure (*from $32*). Hotels charge similar rates for self-parking. For Volcano Bay, park at the main CityWalk garage and transfer to the free shuttle.

From Orlando

Lynx buses 21, 37 and 40 run to the Universal Orlando Resort parking garage (the 40 runs directly from the downtown Orlando Amtrak station). International Drive's I-Ride Trolley stops at Universal Blvd, a half-mile walk from the parks.

Hogwarts Express

A Few Surprises

While Orlando is celebrated for its theme parks, it also harbors a trove of offbeat attractions and hidden gems.

Hide-and-Seek with Mickey Mouse

Silhouettes of the lovable rodent, commonly known as 'Hidden Mickeys', are concealed in everyday spots throughout Walt Disney World®. The history of Hidden Mickeys goes back to the design of Epcot in the early 1980s, when Imagineers began sneaking in undercover Mickey Mouse profiles.

'Hidden Mickeys are especially fun for people who have visited the parks before,' said Steve Barrett, aka the Hidden Mickey Guy. 'They offer an extra layer of appreciation for the care Disney puts in the details. What makes it fun is that the Imagineers add new ones constantly, making finding them an ever-evolving game.'

Walt Disney's Horses

Walt Disney loved horses and he especially enjoyed buzzing around his Burbank studios at the reins of a stagecoach. Disney enlisted the help of Owen and Dolly Pope, a California couple known for their award-winning show horses, to oversee the **Tri-Circle-D Ranch**, home to almost 100 horses and named after the three circles that form the famous Mickey Mouse profile. The ranch is located at the Fort Wilderness Resort and is open during normal working hours; guests are welcome to explore the public areas.

Disney Wilderness Preserve

The Disney Wilderness Preserve near Kissimmee protects 11,500 acres of wetlands and is an essential part of the Everglades ecosystem. Three trails give hikers the chance to see what this area of Florida looked like before Mickey Mouse arrived on the scene.

OFFBEAT ORLANDO

Kayak, snorkel or swim your way through the lush greenery and emerald waters of **Wekiwa Springs State Park** (p121).

Take to the swampy waters of **Lake Tohopekaliga** (p125) on an airboat tour and keep your eye out for all sorts of wildlife.

Paddle a swan-boat through scenic **Lake Eola Park** (p135) and enjoy a picnic under a palm tree.

Learn about African American history at the **Wells' Built Museum** (p134), located in a former hotel.

Airboat, Lake Tohopekaliga (p125)

Wells' Built Museum (p134)

Explore Walt Disney World® Resort

Happily Ever After Nighttime Spectacular, The Magic Kingdom (p44)
DISNEY ©

★ OVERVIEW

Walt Disney World®

Cinderella Castle. Spaceship Earth. Mickey Mouse. And now, an entire land dedicated to Star Wars. Spread across 42 sq miles, Walt Disney World® is a powerful cultural icon that represents the innocence of childhood and the promise of a magically fun time.

PLANNING TIP
The single most useful tool to planning your trip is the My Disney Experience mobile app. From itinerary building to wait times to character meets and restaurant reservations, the app has it all.

Scan this QR code to download the My Disney Experience mobile app.

The Theme Parks

Walt Disney World® is truly a kingdom unto itself: the area includes four walled theme parks and two water parks, all connected by a network of monorail, boats and buses, and intersected by highways and roads. Attractions are spread out among the parks, resort hotels and, to a lesser extent, the entertainment districts.

1 **Magic Kingdom** (p39) is the quintessential Disney experience and the most visited park. 2 **Disney's Hollywood Studios** (p51) brought Pixar into the fold, but its biggest attraction is Star Wars: Galaxy's Edge. 3 **Epcot** (p59) is divided in two: Future World, with rides and interactive exhibits, and World Showcase, providing a toe-dip into global cultures. 4 **Disney's Animal Kingdom** (p69) feels more like a safari than an amusement park and is home to Pandora: The World of Avatar. Two water parks round out the list of amusements and will keep you cool in the stifling summer heat: 5 **Blizzard Beach** (p82) and 6 **Typhoon Lagoon** (p82).

Disney Springs & BoardWalk

The lakeside shopping, dining and entertainment complex of 7 **Disney Springs** (p79) offers a variety of boutiques, restaurants and live performances. Be sure to check out the Marvel Super Hero Headquarters and the Star Wars Galactic Outpost. It's the perfect spot to unwind outside the parks.

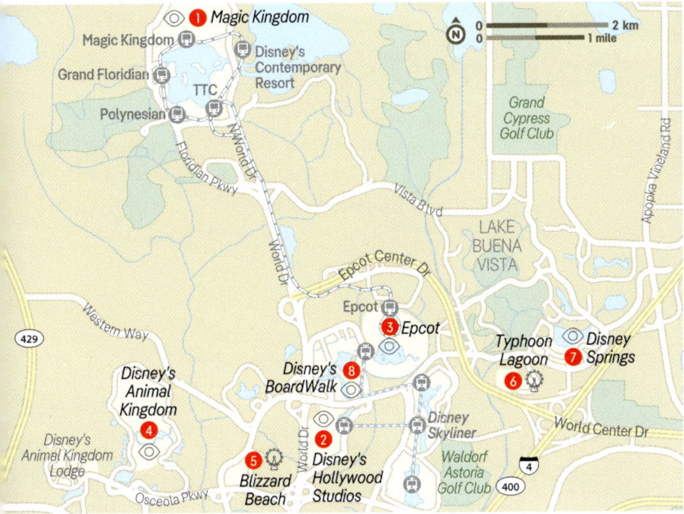

Disney's quarter-mile ❽ **BoardWalk** (p82) is more low-key, with riverside views, street performers and retro fun, making it one of the best stretches to stroll along in Walt Disney World®. It's easily accessible by foot via Epcot's International Gateway.

Getting Around

Budget extra time for getting around (p25). The monorail is an iconic transportation system that connects Magic Kingdom, Epcot and select Disney hotels. The Disney Skyliner connects Epcot and Hollywood Studios, while free boats and buses run to the other parks and resort hotels. Generally, having a car is more hassle than it's worth.

TAKE A BREAK

Throughout the parks, you'll find designated Relaxation Stations where you can sit down and unwind in a shaded area.

★ HISTORY & TIPS

Celebrating Disney

It's been quite a ride since Walt Disney World® first threw open its doors on October 1, 1971. As far-reaching as Walt Disney's imagination was, not even he could have guessed that the park would become part of the very fabric of American culture.

PLANNING TIP
Try to avoid afternoons, which is the hottest and most crowded time of day. Instead, arrive early for the park opening (rope drop) and plan on pool time or a nap at around 3pm or 4pm.

Scan this QR code to purchase tickets to any of the Disney parks.

The Beginning

When Disneyland opened in Southern California in 1955, it fundamentally transformed the concept of theme parks. Walt Disney, however, was irritated with the hotels and concessions that sprung up around the park in a manner he felt was entirely parasitic. Plus, visitor data showed that only 2% of park guests came from east of the Mississippi.

In 1964, after a secret four-year search, Walt Disney bought 27,000 acres of swamp, field and woodland in central Florida. He paid an average of $200 an acre, but once the cat was out of the bag that he was the buyer, the price shot up to $80,000. Disney's vision was to create a family vacation destination wherein he could control every aspect – hotels, restaurants, parking and transportation. It wouldn't just be a theme park, but a 'city of tomorrow', a planned community where people would live and work. At the formal announcement of the plans on November 15, 1965 (nicknamed 'D-Day for Orlando'), Governor Hayden Burns called the date the most significant in the history of Florida.

The Parks

Walt Disney World®'s Magic Kingdom – with Walt's full name added as a tribute – opened in 1971, with the total cost of the project around $400 million.

Star Wars: Galaxy's Edge, Disney's Hollywood Studios (p53)

In the first two years, the park drew 20 million visitors a year, transforming the quiet citrus town of Orlando into the fastest-growing city in the state, the 'Action Center of Florida.'

Epcot – the park that best represented Walt's 'vision of tomorrow' – opened in 1982, followed by Disney-MGM Studios (now Hollywood Studios) and Typhoon Lagoon in 1989. Blizzard Beach opened in 1995 and, three years later, Animal Kingdom. All the while, more than a dozen resorts, a campground and a vast array of recreational facilities, including golf courses, were opening around the parks. Disney Springs first opened in 1975 as the Lake Buena Vista Shopping Village.

The impact of Walt Disney World® cannot be underestimated. It transformed central Florida, and

QUICK BREAK
Mandara Spa at the Swan & Dolphin Hotel promises to take you on a sensory journey, far away from the frenetic energy of Walt Disney World to the heart of Bali.

OPENING HOURS

Opening hours change day to day within any given month. Typical hours are 8am or 9am to between 6pm and 10pm. Magic Hours, for resort guests only, get you in 30 minutes before the crowds.

the arrival of SeaWorld in 1973 and Universal Orlando in 1990 cemented Orlando's new status as the Theme Park Capital of the World. But Walt Disney World® has changed the very nature of theme parks, from a passing attraction into an all-encompassing hermetic experience driven by constant development and innovation. In 2020 Disney was flexing its considerable creative and technological muscle to prepare for its 50th anniversary in 2021, but if the first 50 years are any indication, that effort will continue well into its second half-century of life.

Top Tips for a Successful Disney Vacation

Disney expectations run high, and the reality can be disappointing. Long waits and getting jostled through crowds and lines can exhaust kids and parents.

© DISNEY

Buy tickets that cover more days than you think you'll need. It's less expensive per day and lets you mix theme park time with downtime.

Stay at a Walt Disney World® resort hotel for the convenience offered, though they vary in standards.

Download the My Disney Experience app to see ride wait times, order food, navigate your way around the park, and view listings and shows.

Stock up on snacks to avoid waiting in line for overpriced food or buy a sandwich early for a picnic.

Pimp your stroller with something recognizable so that you can find it easily in the sea of other strollers.

Arrive at the park 30 minutes before gates open and head straight to the most popular rides.

When visiting the Magic Kingdom, factor in travel time from the Transportation & Ticket Center (p25) to the park entrance, which can take up to an hour.

Consider transportation options when booking accommodations; while all Disney resorts offer bus transportation, those with boat and monorail transportation are more convenient (and, except for camping at Fort Wilderness, more expensive).

Manage your kids' expectations by suggesting you're going to spot, rather than meet, a character. Meet-and-greet lines can be extremely long, but you're always likely to see characters in the parades or by chance.

Check for last-minute cancellations to dinner shows or character meals.

SKIP THE LINE

For an additional cost, Disney guests can use the Lightning Lane to bypass long lines. Guests can pay extra to choose from a selection of attractions and experiences, making one selection at a time throughout the day. For more information on Lightning Lane passes (p157).

See p48
for eating,
drinking and
shopping
listings

Explore The Magic Kingdom

Disney mythology comes alive in the Magic Kingdom, starting with Cinderella's fairy-tale castle, inspired by the 1950 animated film. Walkways extend from this hub to the park's six themed lands: Main Street, USA, an old-fashioned shopping district; Adventureland, inspired by Walt's nature documentaries; Frontierland, with a Wild West theme; Liberty Square, focusing on American history; forward-thinking Tomorrowland; and Fantasyland, home to Walt Disney World®'s oldest and most beloved rides as well as the new Storybook Circus. Walt Disney himself oversaw the restoration of the vintage steam trains that loop around the park's 1.5-mile perimeter, making stops at Main Street, Frontierland and Fantasyland.

Getting Around

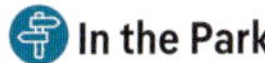

In the Park

Navigating the Magic Kingdom is straightforward with its hub-and-spoke layout centered on Cinderella Castle. The Disney World Railroad, Main Street vehicles and walkways provide easy access.

Getting to the Park

From the Magic Kingdom resorts, you can take a monorail, water taxi or ferry to the park entrance. If you drive, you must park at the Transportation & Ticket Center (p25) and then take the monorail, bus or the ferry to the entrance (allow 45 minutes).

THE BEST

THRILL RIDE Space Mountain (p42)

IMMERSIVE RIDE Haunted Mansion (p42)

DESSERT STOP Plaza Ice Cream Parlour (p49)

FAMILY-FRIENDLY ATTRACTION Jungle Cruise (p43)

SHOP Ye Olde Christmas Shoppe (p49)

Prince Charming Regal Carousel & Cinderella Castle (p42)

DISNEY ©

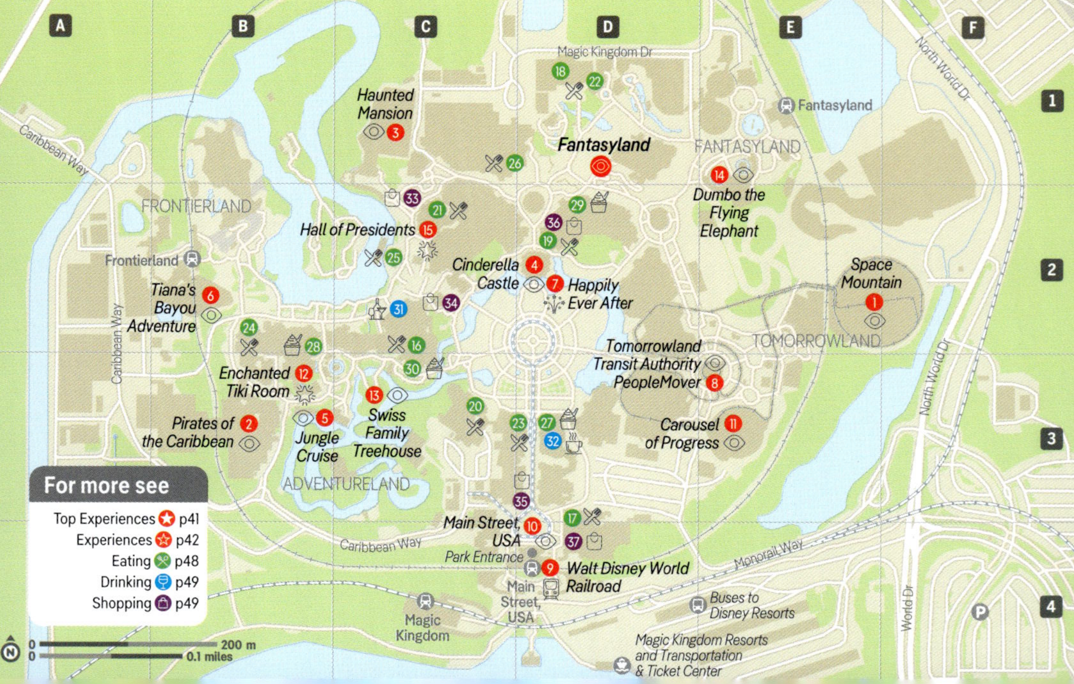
A
B
C
D
E
F
1
2
3
4
Magic Kingdom Dr
Haunted Mansion
3
Fantasyland
Fantasyland
FANTASYLAND
North World Dr
Caribbean Way
26
18
22
14
Dumbo the Flying Elephant
FRONTIERLAND
33
21
29
36
19
Hall of Presidents
15
25
Frontierland
Cinderella Castle
4
7
Happily Ever After
Space Mountain
1
Tiana's Bayou Adventure
6
Caribbean Way
31
34
24
28
16
30
TOMORROWLAND
Tomorrowland Transit Authority PeopleMover
8
Enchanted Tiki Room
12
13
Swiss Family Treehouse
Jungle Cruise
5
Pirates of the Caribbean
2
20
23
27
32
Carousel of Progress
11
North World Dr
ADVENTURELAND
35
Main Street, USA
10
17
37
Caribbean Way
Park Entrance
9
Walt Disney World Railroad
Monorail Way
Main Street, USA
Magic Kingdom
Buses to Disney Resorts
Magic Kingdom Resorts and Transportation & Ticket Center
World Dr
For more see
Top Experiences p41
Experiences p42
Eating p48
Drinking p49
Shopping p49
0 200 m
0 0.1 miles

★ TOP EXPERIENCE

Fantasyland

Iconic Fantasyland opened way back in 1971. Brimming with enchantment, attractions here include it's a small world and Peter Pan's Flight, set against the backdrop of the majestic Cinderella Castle. A 2012 expansion brought new gems like the Seven Dwarfs Mine Train and the captivating Beast's Castle.

MAP: **D1**

Classic Rides

Fantasyland is the spellbinding heart of the Magic Kingdom, especially for the eight-and-under crowd, who love the character-focused experiences.

The classic **it's a small world** boat ride, originally created for the 1964 New York World's Fair, is a whimsical journey through different cultures, featuring the iconic tune. **Peter Pan's Flight** takes you soaring above foggy London and Neverland in a re-creation of the beloved story. The **Seven Dwarfs Mine Train** is a family-friendly roller coaster that combines mild thrills with rich storytelling.

Step into Belle's cottage at **Enchanted Tales with Belle** and you'll be able to participate in the enchanting, interactive retelling of *Beauty and the Beast*. **Under the Sea: Journey of The Little Mermaid** is a captivating dive into Ariel's undersea world. Spin around in giant teacups at the **Mad Tea Party**, a whimsical ride inspired by Alice in Wonderland. It's a fun, dizzying experience for all ages.

Without a doubt the best 3D show in Disney, **Mickey's PhilharMagic**, takes Donald Duck on a fun adventure through classic Disney movies. Ride with him through the streets of Morocco on Aladdin's carpet and feel the champagne on your face when it pops open during *Beauty and the Beast's* Be Our Guest Restaurant (p48).

PLANNING TIP

Consider purchasing a Lightning Lane pass (p157) for expedited access to rides. Prices vary depending on demand and the specific attractions.

Scan this QR code to help plan your trip to Fantasyland.

EXPERIENCES

Blast Off to Space Mountain

THRILL RIDE

MAP: 1 P40 **E2**

Space Mountain, opened in 1975, is one of Disney World's most famous rides. This indoor roller coaster simulates a thrilling journey through outer space, with sharp turns and sudden drops in near-total darkness. The attraction was inspired by Walt Disney's vision of a futuristic spaceport, combining innovative technology and imaginative design. Come first thing or use the Lightning Lane Pass.

Set Sail on Pirates of the Caribbean

FAMILY FRIENDLY

MAP: 2 P40 **B3**

This classic Disney ride, which inspired the hugely successful movie series **Pirates of the Caribbean**, takes guests on a swashbuckling adventure through scenes of pirate lore, featuring lifelike animatronics and memorable characters, like the dastardly Blackbeard and Davy Jones. Sing along with the catchy theme song, 'Yo Ho (A Pirate's Life for Me),' and keep an eye out for the iconic pirate skull-and-crossbones symbol, as well as Captain Jack Sparrow, who might pop up when up when you least expect him. At the end of your swashbuckling adventure, stock up on pirate paraphernalia at the **Plaza del Sol Caribe Bazaar** gift shop, or enjoy a break in the new **Pirate's Lounge**.

Visit the Haunted Mansion

IMMERSIVE ATTRACTION

MAP: 3 P40 **C1**

The Haunted Mansion, one of the Magic Kingdom's original attractions, offers a spooky yet whimsical journey through a ghost-filled manor where 999 happy haunts still live their most merry lives. The vehicles on the ride are called Doom Buggies, clam-shell-shaped carts that glide along a track and offer a 360-degree view of the spooky haunted halls and crypts. As your Doom Buggy enters the seance room, take a closer look at the table where Madame Leota's crystal ball is floating: you might spot a spellbook titled *Grim Grinning Ghosts*, a nod to the iconic song that plays throughout the attraction. Beware of hitchhiking ghosts!

Wish upon a Star at Cinderella Castle

FAMILY FRIENDLY

MAP: 4 P40 **D2**

With its with its elegant spires and intricate details, **Cinderella Castle** looks like it's straight out of a fairy tale. Inspired by Neuschwanstein Castle in Bavaria, Germany, the 189-ft tall Cinderella's Castle, completed in July 1971, stands as an iconic reminder that dreams really do come true if you follow this advice: 'Be kind, have courage and always believe in a little magic.'

Inside the castle, five elaborate glass mosaic murals in the castle's breezeway tell the story of Cinderella, star of the 1950 Disney animated feature film. Designed by Imagineer Dorothea Redmond, the artwork has five 15' x 10' panels made of over 300,000 multicolored tiles made from Italian glass, real silver and 14-karat gold.

Also inside the castle, you'll find the enchanting Cinderella's Royal Table (p48), a dining experience where you can meet a cast of Disney princesses while enjoying a royal feast.

Tinker Bell makes a magical flight from the castle during the nightly fireworks show (p44). She starts her journey by climbing up a tall ladder inside the castle's spire to reach its top window. From there, she uses a zip line to fly over the park, creating a dazzling, don't-miss spectacle.

Enjoy a Riverboat Adventure aboard the Jungle Cruise

FAMILY FRIENDLY

MAP: 5 P40 **B3**

Cruise through exotic locales, where animatronic wildlife abounds on the classic **Jungle Cruise**. Humorous skippers deliver witty commentary, blending thrills and laughs as you journey down rivers inspired by those in Africa, Asia and South America. You'll see elephants splashing in the water, lions watching over their prey and mischievous gorillas causing mayhem. The skippers' puns and jokes add a delightful layer of fun to the experience. By the time you return to the dock, you'll feel as if you've traveled the world in just a few delightful minutes. Several celebrities served as skippers on the Jungle Cruise before finding fame, including Kevin Costner.

Splash Down on Tiana's Bayou Adventure

WATER RIDE

MAP: 6 P40 **B2**

In 2024, **Tiana's Bayou Adventure** transformed Splash Mountain into a journey inspired by *The Princess and the Frog*. This reimagined attraction features music and characters from the film, taking guests on a toe-tapping trip through the shimmering Louisiana bayou. In the queue, you'll discover Tiana's latest business venture, **Tiana's Foods**, an employee-owned

RAPUNZEL'S RESTROOMS

When nature calls, make a beeline for the **Tangled Restrooms**. They're located in **Rapunzel's Tower**, perched atop a rocky cliff with a waterfall. The tower serves as a beacon of sorts, so you can easily identify the location of the guest amenities below. In addition to plentiful restrooms, look for the power-charging stations disguised as tree trunks.

cooperative. Hold on to those beignets and keep your hands inside the boat as you prepare for the exhilarating 50ft drop – those gators have a taste for more than jazz!

End Your Day with the Happily Ever After Fireworks

SHOW

MAP: 7 P40 D2

The grand finale to many a visitor's day in Magic Kingdom is the simply spectacular 20-minute fireworks-and-light show, **Happily Ever After**, that lights up the sky above Cinderella Castle. Images from Disney staples – *Moana*, *Frozen* and *The Lion King* and others – are projected onto the castle walls, all to tell the story of determination and realizing your dreams.

Arrive at least 30 to 45 minutes before the show starts for a better chance of securing a good spot, especially if you're visiting during peak times or holidays.

Take Five on the PeopleMover

FAMILY FRIENDLY

MAP: 8 P40 E3

Crowds got you down? Are your feet aching and your kids about to lose it? Well, there's an escape hatch smack dab in the middle of Tomorrowland, aboard one of the most underrated rides at Disney. The **Tomorrowland Transit Authority PeopleMover** provides an elevated, leisurely tour of the park, with unique views of attractions like Space Mountain and Buzz Lightyear's Space Ranger Spin. It moves at a snail's pace compared to other attractions (about 7mph) – so slow that seatbelts are not required. You'll never wait more than five minutes to board, and the peaceful ride promises 10 minutes of breezy bliss.

The Walt Disney World Railroad

TRANSPORTATION

MAP: 9 P40 D4

The **Walt Disney World® Railroad** offers a delightful 1.5-mile

BEAT THE HEAT IN THE MAGIC KINGDOM

Cool off in the air-conditioned interior and relax your tired feet during a live show, like those at the Enchanted Tiki Room (p46). The Hall of Presidents (p47) and Carousel of Progress (p46) are both over 15 minutes long, with comfortable seating. You can also kick back and catch a breeze aboard the open-air Tomorrowland Transit Authority PeopleMover. Near the entrance to the Jungle Cruise are the so-called Liki Tikis: statues that spray cool mist from their mouths, offering instant relief from the heat. And remember: every food and drink location with a soda fountain gives out free cups of iced water.

journey with three main stops in the Magic Kingdom: Main Street, Frontierland and Fantasyland. Each stop provides a unique gateway to different themed areas, from the nostalgic charm of early 20th-century America to the adventurous Wild West to the enchanting world of fairy tales, making it the most convenient way to explore the diverse attractions of Magic Kingdom.

From the time he was a little boy, Walt Disney loved trains. Perhaps this passion grew via his father, who worked on a track-installation crew for the Union Pacific Railroad, or from his stint as a newspaper, candy and cigar salesman on the Missouri Pacific Railway. He loved trains so much that he built a railroad in his own backyard. The Carolwood Pacific Railroad was a 1/8-scale train pulled by the locomotive *Lilly Belle.*

So when it came to building a railroad that he could share with the world, Disney pulled out all the stops, meticulously restoring four vintage, narrow-gauge steam trains. Many visitors to the Magic Kingdom skip the Walt Disney World® Railroad, a relaxing 20-minute round-trip scenic tour, but it's worth hopping aboard at the Main Street station and enjoying this nostalgic ride around the park.

Stroll down Main Street, USA

FAMILY FRIENDLY

MAP: 10 P40 D4

Main Street, USA, is the charming entrance to Magic Kingdom, designed to transport guests to a nostalgic turn-of-the-century American town. The classic street is lined with quaint shops, restaurants and period architecture, all leading up to the majestic Cinderella Castle (p42). Horse-drawn carriages, vintage cars and a lively atmosphere complete the experience. It's a perfect spot to grab a coffee, enjoy a parade or simply soak in the ambience of yesteryear.

Need a trim on vacay? Harmony Barber Shop is tucked away on the corner of Main Street. This charming barbershop offers haircuts for guests of all ages. One of its delightful traditions is the First Haircut experience for young children, complete with Mickey ears and a certificate.

Meet Your Favorite Disney Characters

MEET & GREET

Fantasyland offers all kinds of excellent character-interaction opportunities. Spend time with Merida in the little stone grotto of **Fairytale Garden**; listen to Belle tell a story at **Enchanted Tales with Belle**; meet Ariel at **Ariel's Grotto** and Gaston by **Gaston's Tavern** (p48); or hop in line and catch a handful of princesses in

Fairytale Hall. And, of course, always keep an eye out for Cinderella, Alice in Wonderland and other favorites hanging out throughout.

On Main Street, you can meet Mickey Mouse, Tinker Bell and her friends from Pixie Hollow at the **Town Square Theater Meet and Greets**.

Note: Mary Poppins is, er, a 'floater'; she appears at different lands at different times. Ask a staff member (known as a 'cast character') where she might be appearing next.

Follow the Carousel of Progress

FAMILY FRIENDLY

MAP: 11 P40 E3

The **Carousel of Progress** is a beloved Disney classic that takes guests on a journey through the 20th century, showcasing the evolution of technology and daily life. Created by Walt Disney himself for the 1964 New York World's Fair, this rotating theater features four acts, each representing a different era. Guests follow the same family as they experience technological advancements, from gas lamps and iceboxes to electric appliances and futuristic gadgets. The show's catchy theme song, 'There's a Great Big Beautiful Tomorrow,' and its optimistic message about progress and innovation, make it a timeless attraction. Try to spot Rover, the family dog: he appears in each of the four acts, subtly changing alongside the family's technological advancements and lifestyle.

Sing Along at the Tiki Room

SHOW

MAP: 12 P40 B3

The **Enchanted Tiki Room** is a delightful, tropical attraction where animatronic birds, flowers and tikis come to life in a lively musical show. Hosted by José, Michael, Fritz and Pierre, the show features a colorful cast of characters singing tunes like 'The Tiki, Tiki, Tiki Room.' The enchanting, light-hearted atmosphere and cool air-con make it a favorite for guests of all ages. Post-show, indulge in a refreshing Dole Whip, an iconic and delicious pineapple soft-serve treat available at nearby Aloha Isle (p49).

Survive a Shipwreck in the Swiss Family Treehouse

FAMILY FRIENDLY

MAP: 13 P40 C3

Explore an elaborate **tree house** inspired by the classic Disney film on this walk-through attraction. A series of interconnected rooms showcases the ingenuity and resourcefulness of the shipwrecked Robinson family. Guests can climb winding staircases, cross rope bridges and discover makeshift furniture, tropical gardens and inventive gadgets, all set amid lush foliage and breathtaking views.

The 60ft tall, 90ft wide, 200-ton tree is botanically classified as *Disneyodendron eximus*, which means 'Extraordinary Disney tree.' While it certainly looks real, it's actually made of steel and concrete.

HAPPIEST OF BIRTHDAYS!

Walt Disney World® cast members love to celebrate birthday boys and girls of all ages. If it's your birthday, pick up a complimentary 'Celebratory Birthday Button' at Guest Relations near the main Magic Kingdom entrance and wear it for a chorus of birthday greetings throughout your magical day. If you're staying at a Disney resort, tell the front desk it's your birthday, and you'll get a special wake-up or goodnight phone call from a Disney character. You can also pre-order a Mickey Mouse birthday cake via the main reservations line, and it will arrive at your table at the restaurant of your choice.

Take to the Skies with Dumbo the Flying Elephant FAMILY FRIENDLY

MAP: 14 P40 E1

Soar through the skies on the back of your own **Dumbo**, everyone's fave flying elephant. When Magic Kingdom opened on October 1, 1971, Dumbo was one of the original attractions; today, it's part of the **Storybook Circus** area, which has a number of attractions geared to the littlest park-goers. Dumbo's colorful, elephant-shaped vehicles gently rise and fall as they circle around a central hub, and riders big and small can control the height of their flight using a lever. The recent addition of a covered, interactive queue area adds to the magic, making the wait time a tad more entertaining.

Post-flight, kids can cool off at **Casey Jr Splash 'N' Soak Station**, a water-play area where the circus animals spray visitors with water and the circus train blows off refreshing 'steam.' Bring swimsuits or a change of clothes as you're guaranteed to get soaked. Minnie Magnifique and Madame Daisy Fortuna love to greet guests at **Pete's Silly Sideshow**. The adjacent **Casey Jr RailRoad Mercantile** sells towels, sunscreen and clothing to replace wet duds.

Watch History Come to Life in the Hall of Presidents SHOW

MAP: 15 P40 C2

The **Hall of Presidents**, in Liberty Square, is a multimedia presentation featuring animatronic figures of every US president, offering a dramatic retelling of the nation's history that brings its leaders to life. Honest Abe kicks off the show with the Gettysburg Address, followed by a speech from George Washington and the oath of office from the current sitting president.

When the Hall of Presidents opened as one of the Magic Kingdom's original attractions, the presidential roll call ended with Richard Nixon. Each newly elected president since then has had an animatronic version of himself added to the show postelection.

LISTINGS

Best Places for...

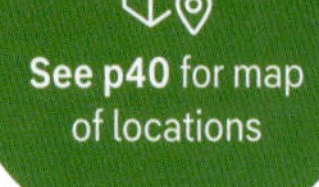
See p40 for map of locations

$ Budget $$ Midrange $$$ Top End

Eating

Sit-Down Restaurants

Jungle Navigation Co Ltd Skipper Canteen $$$

16 C2
When Jungle Cruise skippers aren't navigating treacherous waters they're digging into Asian, South American and African dishes here. *10am-8pm*

Tony's Town Square Restaurant $$$
17 D3
Share a plate of spaghetti and meatballs and re-create the scene from *Lady and the Tramp* beside a fountain depicting the canine couple. *11am-9pm*

Be Our Guest Restaurant $$$
18 D1
Dine in the Beast's castle with a prix-fixe menu featuring French onion soup, coq au vin and a dessert trio. Reserve well ahead. *11am-7pm*

Cinderella's Royal Table $$$
19 D2
Settle in for a regal meal inside Cinderella Castle with princess meet-and-greets and a view of Fantasyland. Reserve well ahead. *11am-7pm*

Crystal Palace $$$
20 C3
A buffet-style restaurant with a jungle theme, offering a variety of American and international dishes. *11am-7pm*

Quick-Service Restaurants

Columbia Harbour House $$

21 C2
A nautical-themed eatery serving seafood favorites like fish sandwiches and lobster rolls. *10:30am-8:30pm*

Gaston's Tavern $
22 D1
A cozy spot that's great for a quick breakfast, offering LeFou's Brew (its signature apple-and-marshmallow drink) and warm cinnamon rolls, with a rustic French tavern ambience. *10am-8pm*

Casey's Corner $

23 D3
A baseball-themed stand serving super-long hot dogs and Cracker Jacks, located at the end of Main Street. *10am-8pm*

Pecos Bill Tall Tale Inn & Cafe $$
24 B2
Serves Tex-Mex classics in Frontierland, from tacos and fajitas to pork carnitas nachos. *7am-11pm*

Turkey Leg Cart $$

25 C2
Another Frontierland standby, come here for the crowd-favorite jumbo turkey legs, cured in a salt solution and reminiscent of smoky ham on the bone. *11am-7pm*

Pinocchio Village Haus $

26 C1
Refuel with quick and easy Italian-American classics like subs, pizza and pasta. *10:30am-9pm*

Sweet Treats

Plaza Ice Cream Parlour $$

27 D3

Settle in under a cute umbrella on the patio and dig into delicious ice-cream delights and perfect views of Cinderella's Castle. Sundaes here are served in freshly made waffle bowls. *7am-11pm*

Aloha Isle $

 B2

Head to Adventureland for the legendary Dole Whip: soft-serve vanilla ice cream with a swirl of pineapple. *10am-8pm*

Storybook Treats $

 D2

Step into a fairy tale of a sweet shop where ice-cream floats entice thirsty princes and princesses. Try the Rapunzel Sundae with wild berry soft-serve. *11am-10pm*

Sunshine Tree Terrace $

 C3

This is the only place in the Magic Kingdom where you'll find the sought-after Orange Bird souvenir sipper, a straw-topped bottle shaped like the adorable bird. *10am-close*

Drinking

Bars & Cafes

Liberty Tree Tavern

 C2

A colonial-themed tavern offering a variety of American dishes and a good selection of beers and wines. *11am-7pm*

Gaston's Tavern

see  D1

Located in Fantasyland, this bar features a fairy-tale atmosphere with a menu of themed drinks and snacks. *11am-7pm*

Main Street Bakery

 D3

Few places are as notorious for bad coffee as the Happiest Place on Earth. Pop into the Main Street Bakery for a charming turn-of-the-century Starbucks. *8:30am-10:30pm*

Shopping

Souvenirs

Memento Mori

 C2

Located near the Haunted Mansion, this spooky shop offers exclusive merchandise, including glassware, spirit jerseys and eerie snacks. *8am-close*

Ye Olde Christmas Shoppe

 C2

On Liberty Square, this festive store offers holiday decorations and ornaments year-round, ensuring you can bring the magic of Christmas home anytime. *9am-close*

Emporium

 D3

The largest gift and souvenir shop in Magic Kingdom, located on Main Street, with a wide selection of Disney-themed merchandise. *9am-11pm*

Sir Mickey's

 D2

Offers a delightful selection of costumes, apparel, and accessories for all ages, making it a perfect spot to find souvenirs and dress-up items. *8am-6pm*

Curtain Call Collectibles

37 D4

Get your traditional Mickey ears customised with on-the-spot embroidery off Main Street. Look around and see if you can spot the references to the 1947 animated short *Mickey and the Beanstalk*. *9am-11pm*

See p57
for eating, drinking and shopping listings

Explore Disney's Hollywood Studios

Disney's Hollywood Studios, which opened in 1989, brings the silver-screen magic to Walt Disney World®. The park is divided into seven themed areas inspired by real-life LA film locations or cinematic worlds. The main landmark is a replica of Grauman's Chinese Theatre, home to Mickey & Minnie's Runaway Railway. Star Wars: Galaxy's Edge and Toy Story Land introduce high-tech attractions like Star Wars: Rise of the Resistance, considered one of the park's best rides, and Toy Story Midway Mania. This blend of old and new creates a unique, immersive experience for all visitors.

Getting Around

Getting There

The park is well-connected to the rest of Disney via walkways, buses, the Disney Skyliner and boats from nearby resorts.

On Foot

Navigating Disney's Hollywood Studios is a breeze: follow the themed areas via clearly marked signs. For a smoother visit, plan your day around Lightning Lane reservations and entertainment schedules.

Wheelchairs & Strollers

Rentals are available near the entrance.

THE BEST

THRILL RIDE Tower of Terror (p54)

CAPTIVATING SHOW *Fantasmic!* (p55)

DESSERT STOP Hollywood Scoops (p56)

SHOP Tatooine Traders (p57)

Mickey & Minnie's Runaway Railway (p54)

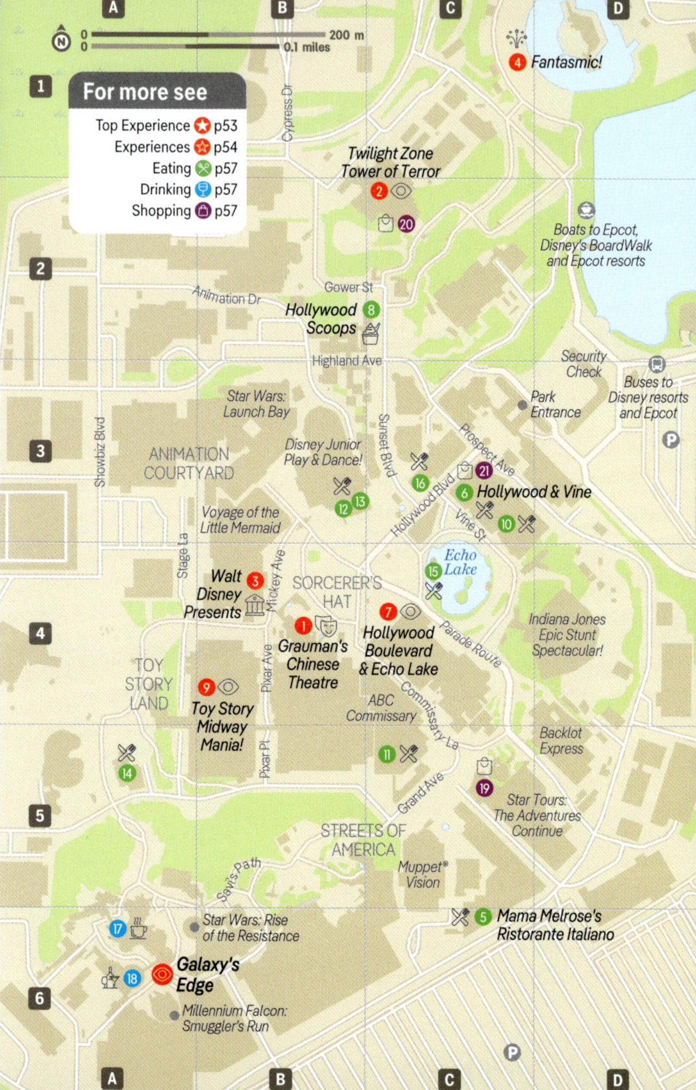
A
B
C
D
200 m
0.1 miles
For more see
Top Experience p53
Experiences p54
Eating p57
Drinking p57
Shopping p57
Fantasmic!
Cypress Dr
Twilight Zone Tower of Terror
Boats to Epcot, Disney's BoardWalk and Epcot resorts
Animation Dr
Gower St
Hollywood Scoops
Highland Ave
Security Check
Park Entrance
Buses to Disney resorts and Epcot
Star Wars: Launch Bay
Showbiz Blvd
ANIMATION COURTYARD
Disney Junior Play & Dance!
Sunset Blvd
Prospect Ave
Hollywood Blvd
Hollywood & Vine
Vine St
Voyage of the Little Mermaid
Stage La
Echo Lake
Walt Disney Presents
Mickey Ave
SORCERER'S HAT
Grauman's Chinese Theatre
Hollywood Boulevard & Echo Lake
Parade Route
Indiana Jones Epic Stunt Spectacular!
TOY STORY LAND
Toy Story Midway Mania!
Pixar Ave
ABC Commissary
Commissary La
Backlot Express
Pixar Pl
Grand Ave
Star Tours: The Adventures Continue
STREETS OF AMERICA
Muppet® Vision
Savi's Path
Mama Melrose's Ristorante Italiano
Star Wars: Rise of the Resistance
Galaxy's Edge
Millennium Falcon: Smuggler's Run

★ TOP EXPERIENCE

Star Wars: Galaxy's Edge

Disney's 14-acre Black Spire Outpost on Batuu is Disney's most ambitious technological feat yet. Every detail, from the architecture to the life-sized Millennium Falcon and live performances, is truly impressive. The two standout rides set a new bar in immersive theme park design.

MAP: **A6**

Board the Millennium Falcon

Hop aboard the iconic **Millennium Falcon** and team up with two pilots, two gunners and two engineers to fly the 'fastest hunk of junk in the galaxy' on a daring mission. While the immersive video-game experience involves pressing a lot of buttons, the thrill of being inside a full-scale version of Han and Chewy's ship is undeniable.

Become a Jedi aboard Star Wars: Rise of the Resistance

This isn't just a ride – it's a 20-minute, multi-part **high-tech adventure** that combines four different ride systems and a stunning walkthrough experience. As a crew member on a captured transport, you'll have to escape the First Order after being tractor-beamed into an Imperial Star Destroyer.

Immerse Yourself in the Story at Black Spire Outpost

Engage with the live actors and participate in the interactive elements scattered throughout Black Spire Outpost. Chat with the locals, try out the themed food and drinks, and let yourself be part of the Star Wars adventure.

PLANNING TIP
Head to **Savi's Workshop** or **Mubo's Droid Depot** early in the day to book a spot to build your own lightsaber or droid; these activities fill up quickly.

Scan this QR code to help plan your trip to the Galaxy's Edge.

EXPERIENCES

Visit Grauman's Chinese Theatre & the Runaway Railway

FAMILY FRIENDLY

MAP: 1 P52 **B4**

Just like the original Grauman's (now TCL) Chinese Theatre in Hollywood, this Disneyfied theater is home to a forecourt featuring the signatures and hand- and footprints of the biggest and brightest stars of all time. Disney's version of **Grauman's Chinese Theatre** is an exact replica, right down to the two giant lions, aka heavenly guard dogs, that stand at full attention at the entrance.

The theater holds **Mickey & Minnie's Runaway Railway**, a trackless dark ride inspired by the rodent duo's animated shorts. Step inside a cartoon world inhabited by Disney's earliest animated friends as you ride off on the train. It's also the first ride at any Disney park that stars Mickey Mouse.

At night the theater's iconic facade flickers with projected scenes of memorable Disney moments. The 10-minute journey through Disney movie history features both beloved characters and villains, and ends with a recording of Walt Disney reminding everyone, 'It was all started by a mouse.'

Descend into the Twilight Zone

THRILL RIDE

MAP: 2 P52 **C2**

On your tour of a now decrepit Hollywood hotel, the **Tower of Terror** elevator taking you up to the 13th floor experiences a series of strange events... Inspired by *The Twilight Zone*, this brilliantly executed ride recalls Hollywood's Golden Age. Passengers experience multiple freefall drops at 39 mph, revealing a bird's-eye view of the park. A camera captures passengers' fear as they freefall.

Zoom Away on Slinky Dog Dash

FAMILY FRIENDLY

Shrink down to toy-size and hitch a ride on *Toy Story*'s Slinky Dog (p56, *see* 9). Reaching speeds of up to 40 mph, this family-friendly ride is filled with twists, turns, and impeccable theming. There aren't any inversions, loops, or freefalls, so it's perfect for more casual roller coaster riders.

Along with Star Wars: Rise of the Resistance (p53), **Slinky Dog Dash** is one of the most popular rides in the park. Prepare to wait 90+ minutes mostly outdoors or splurge on a Lightning Lane Multi Pass (p157) to skip the line.

Delve into Disney History at Walt Disney Presents

INTERACTIVE MUSEUM

MAP: 3 P52 **B4**

This immersive exhibit at Hollywood Studios showcases the life and legacy of Walt Disney. Visitors can see rare artifacts, original sketches and detailed models of Disney's greatest creations. The exhibit includes a 15-minute film highlighting Walt's journey from a small-town boy to the creative genius behind some of the country's most beloved characters and stories. It's a fascinating glimpse into the history and innovation that built the magic of Disney parks. To become an official Disney historian, ask a cast member if you can take 'the test.' Answer the series of Disney-related questions correctly and you'll be awarded an honorary certificate.

See Soaring Fireworks in Fantasmic! SHOW

Fantasmic! (MAP: 4 P52 C1) at Disney's Hollywood Studios is a spectacular nighttime show that features Mickey Mouse battling Disney villains in a dream-like sequence. The show includes incredible water projections, pyrotechnics and live performances set to a magical musical score. Get to the Hollywood Hills Amphitheater at least 30 to 60 minutes before the show to secure a good spot. Aim for seats in the amphitheater's middle section for the best action views and special effects. As an outdoor show, *Fantasmic!* can be affected by weather conditions. In case of rain, be prepared with ponchos or umbrellas.

Also consider the dining package, which includes a meal at restaurants like **50's Prime Time Café** (p57, *see* 10), **Mama Melrose's Ristorante Italiano** (MAP: 5 P52 C6) or **Hollywood & Vine** (MAP: 6 P52 C3), as well as a voucher for guaranteed seating in a reserved section.

BEST STAGE SHOWS AT DISNEY'S HOLLYWOOD STUDIOS

For the First Time in Forever: A Frozen Sing-Along Celebration
'Let It Go' with ice princess Elsa at this sing-along stage show.

Beauty & the Beast Live on Stage
Settle in for a tale as old as time at this timeless musical show.

Disney Movie Magic
This nightly spectacular lights up Grauman's Chinese Theatre with projections of classic movie moments – the perfect way to wrap up a cinematic day in the park.

Stroll with the Stars on Hollywood Boulevard SHOP

Hollywood Boulevard (MAP: 7 P52 C4) at Disney's Hollywood Studios transports you to 1930s Hollywood with its vintage architecture, neon signs and classic movie posters. Leading up to the majestic Chinese Theatre, the boulevard is lined with charming shops selling Disney merchandise, delightful places to eat and a Starbucks to keep you caffeinated. Throughout the day, you'll encounter lively street performers and parades, so keep your eyes peeled for iconic actors

DISNEY CHARACTER MEET-&-GREETS

Meet-and-greet characters and times are subject to change; always check the **My Disney Experience** app or **Times Guide** on the day of your visit. Olaf meets guests behind the Hyperion Theater, home of the Frozen Sing-Along (p55). Sulley from Monsters, Inc, can often be found at the rear of Walt Disney Presents (p54), near the Animation Courtyard. Mickey and Minnie are dressed to impress at Red Carpet Dreams, near the entrance of the Sci-Fi Dine-in Theater Restaurant. Woody and Buzz can be found at Woody's Picture Shootin' Corral at Pixar Place. The goofy Green Army Men are often around, too.

like Marilyn Monroe, who often make surprise appearances. One shop worth visiting on Hollywood Boulevard is Mickey's of Hollywood, where you'll find a wide range of character apparel, plush toys and unique collectibles. For a quick snack, stop by **Hollywood Scoops** (MAP: 8 P52 **C2**) for delicious ice cream treats or the Trolley Car Café, where you can grab a coffee along with some tasty pastries and sandwiches. It's the perfect place to soak in the Hollywood magic, snap memorable photos with various characters and kick off your day of fun and excitement at the park.

Toy Story Midway Mania!

FAMILY FRIENDLY

MAP: 9 P52 **B4**

Everything is oversized in Toy Story Land – but that's because you've been shrunk to the size of a toy and are now in Andy's backyard, where you can play with all the other toys from the Toy Story universe.

Don your 3D glasses for **Midway Mania!**, which transports you to Andy's toy box. From inside your car you'll shoot at carnival targets to rack up points.

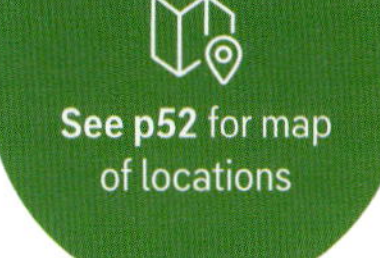
See p52 for map of locations

Best Places for...

$ Budget $$ Midrange $$$ Top End

Eating

Sit-Down Restaurants

50's Prime Time Café $$$
10 C3
Classic American comfort food, '50s kitsch and an old-fashioned family gathering take you back to a bygone era. *11am-close*

Sci-Fi Dine-In Theater $$$
11 C5
1950s-style drive-in theater, featuring all-American favorites served to diners seated in vintage cars. *10:30am-9pm*

Hollywood Brown Derby $$$
12 B3
Serves the same timeless dishes that once graced the celeb-filled tables at the Hollywood original. *11am-9pm*

Bamboo Room $$$

13 B3
Learn what it takes to dream up a Disney World attraction with a Disney Imagineer. By reservation only (1-407-WDW-DINE).

Quick-Service Restaurants

Woody's Lunch Box $$
14 A5
A walk-up restaurant serving gourmet takes on classic kiddie favorites. *8:30am-9pm*

Min & Bill's Dockside Diner $$
15 C4
Quick-service food stand paying tribute to the 1930 MGM comedy-drama *Min and Bill*. *9am-8pm*

Trolley Car Café $$
16 C3
Grab your favorite Starbucks drink and pastry for a breakfast on-the-go. *7am-10pm*

Drinking

Star Wars Cantinas

Milk Stand
17 A6
Sip on Batuu's legendary blue or green milk, served frozen in a Star Wars setting. *9am-10pm*

Oga's Cantina

18 A6
A lively spaceport cantina that welcomes guests from all corners of the galaxy, serving intergalactic drinks like the Jedi Mind Trick. *9am-9pm*

Shopping

Souvenirs

Tatooine Traders

19 C5
Shop for Star Wars memorabilia, build your own lightsaber and browse through rare collectibles. *7am-11pm*

Tower Hotel Gifts
20 C2
Find thrilling gifts and unique souvenirs inspired by *The Twilight Zone*. *7am-11pm*

Mickey's of Hollywood
21 C3
Time-travel with Mickey from the 1920s to the 1940s and pick up Disney-themed keepsakes. *7am-11pm*

See p67
for eating, drinking and shopping listings

Explore Epcot

Walt Disney's dream for the Experimental Prototype Community of Tomorrow (Epcot) was a forward-thinking city. After his death, the city concept was replaced and in 1982 Epcot opened as a theme park, with Spaceship Earth as its symbol. The park is divided into four neighborhoods: World Showcase, World Celebration, World Nature and World Discovery. World Showcase has 11 country pavilions, such as Norway's Frozen Ever After and France's Ratatouille. World Nature and World Discovery offer STEM-focused rides like Test Track and Mission: Space. Epcot is more soothingly low-key than other parks, and has some of Disney's best food and shopping.

Getting Around

Entrance

Enter Epcot through the International Gateway by Disney's Beach Club Resort for shorter lines. Use FriendShip Boats or the Disney Skyliner for scenic, convenient travel between Epcot, Hollywood Studios and the resorts. Boarding docks are at the World Showcase entrance and the Morocco pavilion.

On Foot

Epcot spans 305 acres (approximately 0.476 sq miles), so you'll be doing lots of walking; wear comfortable shoes. Use the My Disney Experience app to check wait times, make dining reservations and manage your itinerary.

Test Track and Spaceship Earth (p63)

THE BEST

IMMERSIVE RIDE Soarin' Around the World (p63)

THRILL RIDE Test Track (p63)

GENTLE RIDE Living with the Land (p64)

HIDDEN HOTSPOT La Cava del Tequila (p66)

FESTIVAL Epcot's International Flower & Garden Festival (p64)

A B C D
1 2 3 4 5 6

0 200 m
0 0.1 miles

For more see

Top Experiences p61
Experiences p63
Eating p67
Drinking p67
Shopping p67

Epcot
Security Check
Epcot Ticket Booths
Tramway
Avenue of the Stars
7 Seas with Nemo & Friends Pavilion
1 Spaceship Earth
8 Guardians of the Galaxy Cosmic Rewind
Play! Pavilion
9 Journey of the Water
6 Living with the Land
FUTURE WORLD
5 Mission: Space
2 Test Track
3 Soarin' Around the World
Imagination Pavilion
Odyssey Center
Mexico Pavilion
Canada Pavilion
World Showcase Prom
World Showplace Events Pavilion
23
20
11
La Cava del Tequila
4 Frozen Ever After
Norway Pavilion
High St
21
16
14
World Showcase
13
China Pavilion
18
World Showcase Lagoon
America Gardens Theatre
22
Germany Pavilion
Morocco Pavilion
17
19
Mitsukoshi Department Store
10
12
Japan Pavilion
American Adventure Pavilion
Italy Pavilion
15

★ TOP EXPERIENCE

World Showcase

Who needs the hassle of jet lag when you can travel the world right here? The **World Showcase** features 11 international pavilions surrounding a lagoon. Watch belly dancing in Morocco, eat pizza in Italy and buy perfume in France, before settling down to watch the fireworks.

MAP **B5**

It's a Small World

Seasoned travelers may scoff at the ersatz quality of it all, but so what? The idea here is to prompt you to hop on a plane and explore the real thing; in the meantime, this is a fun way to show kids a little something about the world.

The best way to experience the World Showcase is to simply wander as the mood moves you, poking through stores and restaurants, and catching what amounts to Bureau of Tourism promotional films and gentle rides through some of the countries.

Highlights

Start your day with croissants at Les Halles Boulangerie & Patisserie in the **France** pavilion, then take a 4D whirl aboard Remy's Ratatouille Adventure. The **Mexico** pavilion's Mesoamerican pyramid towers over the lagoon and houses a restaurant with a twilight market backdrop and the Three Caballeros, a boat ride through Mexico led by Donald Duck.

Meet Anna and Elsa at the Royal Sommerhus in the **Norway** pavilion and set off on another boat journey through Arendelle on Frozen Ever After. In the **China** pavilion, a replica of Beijing's Temple

PLANNING TIP

You can cross the World Showcase Lagoon at Epcot by taking one of the FriendShip Boats, which provide a scenic ride between key points around the lagoon.

Scan this QR code to help plan your trip to the World Showcase.

Morocco Pavilion exterior with Friendship Boat

TAKE A BREAK
La Cantina de San Angel in the Mexico pavilion is one of the best fast-food options in the park. It serves tacos with tasty pico de gallo (fresh salsa), nachos, margaritas and more.

of Heaven offers an immersive Circle-Vision 360-degree visit to the Middle Kingdom. The **Germany** pavilion's Biergarten Restaurant re-creates an open-air beer garden at dusk, while the Via Napoli Ristorante in the **Italy** pavilion serves wood-fired Neapolitan pizzas; look for the Venetian gondolas docked on the lakefront.

Snack on edamame and *kakigōri* at the **Japan** pavilion's Kabuki Café, or strike a pose with Aladdin and Jasmine at the **Morocco** pavilion. Get a glimpse of Alice in Wonderland at the **UK** pavilion, or stock up on maple syrup and NHL apparel at Northwest Mercantile. There's a patriotic audio-animatronic show in the **USA** pavilion, celebrating America's history with inspired storytelling.

EXPERIENCES

Enter Spaceship Earth

FAMILY FRIENDLY

MAP: 1 P60 **B2**

It took almost two years to construct the 180ft-tall, 8000-ton **Spaceship Earth**, the first large-scale geodesic sphere ever. Spaceship Earth isn't just an architectural icon – it also houses an attraction of the same name, which takes guests on a 15-minute ride through time, in vehicles traveling along a track that spirals up to the top of the sphere. Science fiction writer Ray Bradbury, author of *The Martian Chronicles*, helped write the original storyline for the ride. In a 1982 interview with *OMNI* magazine, Bradbury shared his thoughts on the park: 'What Disney is doing is showing the world that there are alternative ways to do things that can make us all happy. If we can borrow some of the concepts of Disneyland and Disney World and Epcot, then indeed the world can be a better place.'

Design Your Own Virtual Car

THRILL RIDE

MAP: 2 P60 **C3**

Create your own car and put it to the test at **Test Track**, where you can see how it performs in extreme heat, cold, high speeds, sudden stops and wicked crashes. The experience simulates the tests conducted on real-life concept cars by leading drivers. You'll zoom through sharp turns and accelerate on straightaways, but watch out for that huge semi with blinding lights! This is the fastest ride at Walt Disney World® Resort, reaching speeds of up to 65 mph.

Soar Around the World

IMMERSIVE RIDE

MAP: 3 P60 **D3**

Buckle up and get ready to lift off on a hang glider, as you soar over the continents and some of the world's most iconic landmarks. **Soarin' Around the World** is a flight simulator attraction that takes guests on a breathtaking journey over some of the world's most iconic landmarks and natural wonders. Arguably the most inspiring ride at Epcot, Soarin' brings the world to you. Using a mechanical lift system and an 80-foot IMAX digital projection dome, it genuinely creates the illusion of hang gliding, complete with wind effects to enhance the experience. Though this flight promises zero turbulence, ask to be seated to the far right in the back row if you have a fear of heights. Hit this one first thing in the morning.

Take a Ride with Elsa and Anna

FAMILY FRIENDLY

MAP: 4 P60 **C4**

The hottest ride in the World Showcase (p61) is in the Norway pavilion: a *Frozen*-themed slow-boat journey aboard a dragon-headed longboat. **Frozen Ever After** features all your favorite tunes and animatronic characters and scenes from the movie, including a visit to Elsa's ice palace and an encounter with Marshmallow, the giant snowman. The cold definitely won't bother you.

Rocket to Mars aboard Mission: SPACE

IMMERSIVE RIDE

MAP: 5 P60 D3

The year is 2036 and you're a test pilot at the International Space Training Center. You're assigned a seat in the four-person launch capsule. 3-2-1-Liftoff!

Mission: Space simulates a thrilling mission to Mars, using centrifugal force to create a realistic sense of space travel, including zero-gravity weightlessness. Guests can choose between the more intense Orange Mission (motion sickness possible) or the milder Green Mission. Both incorporate interactive elements and realistic special effects.

Learn about Sustainable Farming at Living with the Land

FAMILY FRIENDLY

MAP: 6 P60 A3

Set off on an educational boat ride through various agricultural scenes, innovative greenhouses and diverse ecosystems from rainforests to deserts and prairies. **Living with the Land** showcases cutting-edge techniques used to grow crops sustainably, including hydroponics and aquaculture. You'll also get a behind-the-scenes look at Disney's experimental horticulture projects, which supply fresh produce to Epcot restaurants. Be on the lookout for the incredible Mickey-shaped pumpkins!

The Living with the Land **Behind the Seeds Tour** whisks visitors behind the scenes for a one-hour tour of the fish farm and four greenhouses that make up the Land pavilion. Learn more about the catfish and freshwater shrimp that make their way from the fish farm to restaurants around

EPCOT'S FLOWER & GARDEN FESTIVAL

Every spring, Epcot bursts into bloom during its nearly three-month-long **International Flower & Garden Festival**. While the Epcot landscapes are always a delight, this cherished festival elevates the gardens to the next level. The Disney-character-shaped topiaries that pop up across the park are true 'shrubs of art,' with new characters appearing on the green scene every year. A few favorite topiaries also return year after year, including Tinker Bell, who wears a dress made from reindeer moss. Hundreds of butterflies flutter into the festival's Goodness Garden Butterfly House, where you just might see chrysalises transforming into butterflies.

Walt Disney World®, discover new plant-growing techniques and learn the secrets behind raising mega-sized, Disney-character-shaped fruits and vegetables. You'll even get to sample a fruit or veggie grown on-site. Reserve your spot on the tour, which is offered multiple times a day, on the My Disney Experience app. This is a one-hour walking tour, so wear comfortable shoes.

Swim Through the Seas with Nemo & Friends FAMILY FRIENDLY

MAP: 7 P60 **B2**

Kids under 10 won't want to miss the Nemo-themed attractions at Epcot's Future World. Hop aboard a clamobile in the **Seas with Nemo & Friends** and dive into the ocean on an underwater adventure. This gentle ride ends with an impressive aquarium exhibit, blending animated projections with real marine life for an educational and entertaining experience.

Hop Aboard Guardians of the Galaxy: Cosmic Rewind IMMERSIVE RIDE

MAP: 8 P60 **B2**

Guardians of the Galaxy: Cosmic Rewind has quickly become one of the most beloved rides in Epcot since its opening in 2022. Part of the reason is all of the ride's superlatives – it's Disney's first Omnicoaster, a ride with rotating ride vehicles (instead of rotating platforms); Disney's first reverse launch coaster; and one of the largest fully indoor roller coasters on the planet!

Beyond all of that, this ride seamlessly blends thrills and a storyline. We won't spoil the plot, but it's safe to say that you'll, well, be saving the universe (it is Guardians of the Galaxy, after all), with a great soundtrack to boot.

Feel the Power of the Ocean at Journey of Water IMMERSIVE WALK

MAP: 9 P60 **B2**

Inspired by Moana, **Journey of Water** seems like a simple walking trail at first glance, but it's so much more. While on this lush path, you'll get to interact with – and even seemingly control – the water, just like Moana herself, while also learning about the water cycle. With fountains, rivers, and even a 'water harp', it's edutainment at its finest.

Harvest Pearls at the Mitsukoshi Department Store SHOP

MAP: 10 P60 **B2**

Housed in a sprawling, two-story building reminiscent of an imperial ceremonial hall, the Japan pavilion's **Mitsukoshi Department Store** in the World Showcase (p61) offers more than shopping till you drop. Separated into four key zones named Festivity, Silence, Harmony and Interest, this location is the only outpost of the department store to be found outside of Japan. Its first

TAKE A TEQUILA FLIGHT TO MEXICO

MAP: 11 P60 **C4**

The Mexico pavilion's Mesoamerican pyramid in the World Showcase conceals the **Plaza de los Amigos**, a traditional village and marketplace where it's always a starry night. **La Cava del Tequila**, located next to to the San Angel Inn Restaurante, recalls a hidden hacienda with its small cellar charm, rich leather seats and worn walls adorned with original artifacts that showcase the rich tradition of tequila making, including murals that depict the intricate transformation from agave plant to spirit. There are over 100 fine varieties to choose from, including intense blancos, complex reposados and velvety smooth añejos.

incarnation was established in Tokyo in 1673! It's filled with imported items rarely sold in the USA, including green tea Kit-Kat bars, traditional kimonos, hand-painted sun umbrellas and every flavor of marble-capped Ramune soda under the sun. Disney characters share shelf space here with the iconic characters of Japan, such as Hello Kitty and Pikachu.

One pop-up shop located within the always bustling store pays tribute to the the Ama divers, the sea women of Japan, who have been free-diving for pearls for over 3000 years. At the **Pick a Pearl** station, guests can hand-pick their own oyster from an aquarium and pry it open to discover a pearl of their own. If it's a plump pearl, expect the cast members to beat a taiko drum in celebration.

Drink Around the World

EAT & DRINK

While a simple stroll around **Epcot's World Showcase** (p61) is perfectly pleasant, some guests like to take things up a notch by drinking around the world. Some crowd favorites include the violet sake (*$9*) from The Garden House in the Japan pavilion, the grand marnier orange slush (*$14.95*) at Le Vins de Chefs de France in the French pavilion, and the Dos Hombres Avocado (*$19.50*) – better known as the avocado margarita – at La Cava del Tequila in the Mexico Pavilion.

While some participants aim to try one drink from each of the 11 countries, that's not something we recommend.

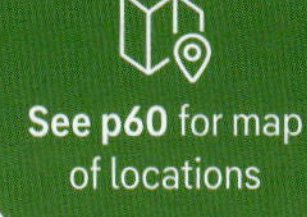
See p60 for map of locations

Best Places for...

$ Budget $$ Midrange $$$ Top End

Eating

Sit-Down Restaurants

Katsura Grill $$
12 B6
Choose from sushi, ramen and udon in a tranquil Japanese garden. *10:30am-close*

Nine Dragons Restaurant $$$
13 D5
Savor contemporary Chinese cuisine amid ornate wood carvings, traditional lanterns and exquisite glass artwork. *11am-9pm*

Rose & Crown $$$
14 A5
This British pub serves traditional favorites and has evening entertainment. *11am-10pm*

Via Napoli $$$
15 C6
Enjoy authentic Neapolitan pizza cooked in wood-burning ovens, along with pasta, salad and gelato. *11am-10pm*

Quick-Service Restaurants

Yorkshire County Fish Shop $$
16 A5
Savor battered fish served with piping-hot chips (fries). *11am-9pm*

Kabuki Cafe $$

17 B6
Cool off with *kakigōri* (shaved ice flavored with syrup and condensed milk) in the Japan pavilion. *11am-9pm*

Drinking

Bars

Champagne Kiosk
18 A5
Toast the day with bubbly at this belle-epoque stand at the France pavilion. *noon-9pm*

Fife & Drum Tavern
19 B6
Sip on American cocktails, like the Frozen Red Stag Lemonade, in a red-white-and-blue setting. *11am-9pm*

Choza de Margarita
20 C4
Enjoy refreshing margaritas and Mexican snacks at this lively outdoor bar. *11am-9pm*

Shopping

Souvenirs

The Tea Caddy
21 A5
This quaint shop has a variety of tea blends, biscuits and Alice in Wonderland–inspired housewares. *10am-9pm*

Karamell-Küche
22 C6
Choose from an array of caramel treats, made daily on-site. Inspired by a Black Forest confectionary. *11am-9pm*

Plaza de los Amigos
23 C4
Come to this bustling Mexican village for handcrafted ceramics, jewelry and *Coco*-inspired merch. *11am-9pm*

See p77 for eating, drinking and shopping listings

Explore Disney's Animal Kingdom

Around 2000 animals representing 300 species of wildlife, from Sumatran tigers to gorillas, live in Disney's Animal Kingdom. It's half-theme park, half-zoo, and it's the greenest, most immersive and calmest of all the parks. Spot African animals from open-sided vehicles on Kilimanjaro Safaris, see James Cameron's 2009 film to life with breathtaking visuals at Pandora: The World of Avatar brings and take to Expedition Everest, which climbs to the peak of the Forbidden Mountain where a yeti lurks. The park's Tree of Life symbolizes the mystical circle that connects all living beings. The animals are most active in the mornings, so arrive early.

Getting Around

Getting There

Disney buses stop at Animal Kingdom, but be warned that the ride here can take up to 45 minutes. There is parking just outside the entrance gates.

On Foot

Navigating Disney's Animal Kingdom is straightforward, with the park organized into six themed lands connected by pathways radiating from the central Discovery Island, which features the Tree of Life.

Wheelchairs & Strollers

Rentals are available near the entrance.

THE BEST

IMMERSIVE RIDE Avatar: Flight of Passage (p71)

ANIMAL-BASED ATTRACTION Kilimanjaro Safaris (p73)

THRILL RIDE Expedition Everest (p74)

SHOW Festival of the Lion King (p74)

FAMILY-FRIENDLY ATTRACTION Rafiki's Planet Watch (p76)

Tree of Life (p73)

DISNEY ©

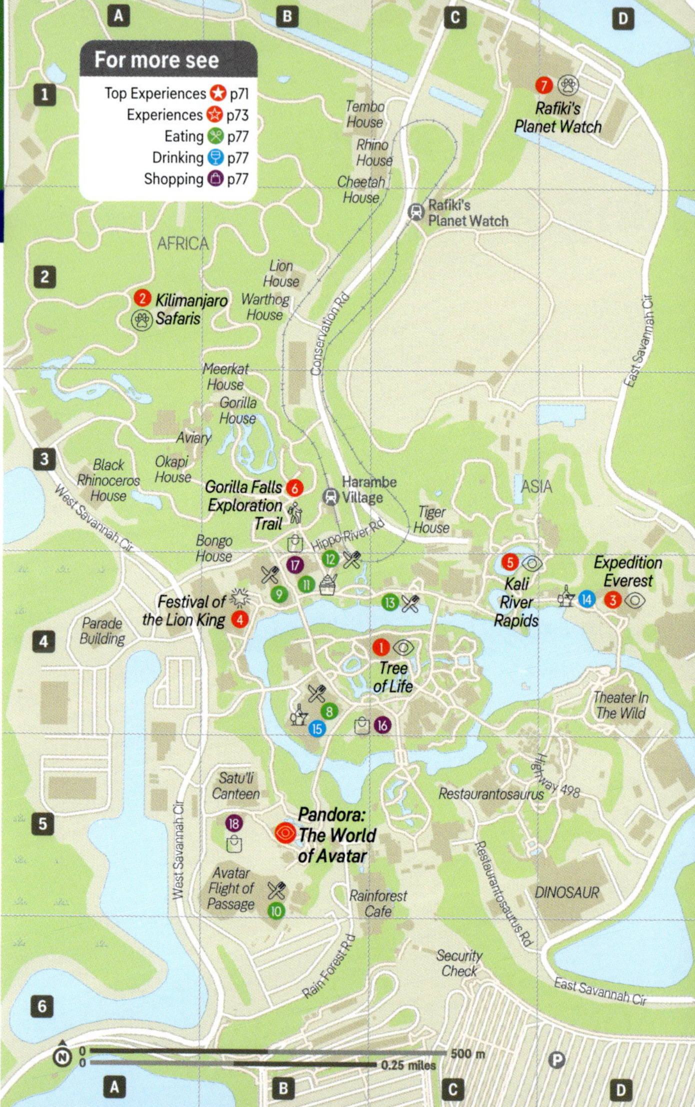
For more see
Top Experiences p71
Experiences p73
Eating p77
Drinking p77
Shopping p77
Tembo House
Rhino House
Cheetah House
Rafiki's Planet Watch
7 Rafiki's Planet Watch
AFRICA
Lion House
Warthog House
2 Kilimanjaro Safaris
Conservation Rd
East Savannah Cir
Meerkat House
Gorilla House
Aviary
Okapi House
Black Rhinoceros House
West Savannah Cir
Gorilla Falls Exploration Trail 6
Harambe Village
Hippo River Rd
Tiger House
ASIA
Bongo House
5 Kali River Rapids
Expedition Everest 3
Festival of the Lion King 4
Parade Building
1 Tree of Life
Theater In The Wild
Highway 498
Restaurantosaurus
Satu'li Canteen
Pandora: The World of Avatar
West Savannah Cir
Restaurantosaurus Rd
Avatar Flight of Passage
Rainforest Cafe
DINOSAUR
Security Check
Rain Forest Rd
East Savannah Cir
0 500 m
0 0.25 miles

★ TOP EXPERIENCE

Pandora: The World of Avatar

Pandora: The World of Avatar features otherworldly landscapes, thrilling attractions and immersive experiences. This alien-like area, opened in May 2017, brings James Cameron's cinematic vision to life, offering visitors an unforgettable journey through the world of Pandora.

MAP **B5**

The Valley of Mo'ara

Welcome to the Valley of Mo'ara, where floating islands and the beautifully lush vegetation leave you in no doubt that this is a land far away from Earth – 4.3 light years away, to be exact. Drift slowly through the stunningly detailed bioluminescent forest on the Na'vi River Journey (p72) or soar through Pandora atop a banshee on Avatar: Flight of Passage.

Avatar buffs will note that the setting is connected to Pandora long after the events of the film: the Na'vi and the humans are now collaborating to protect Pandora's fragile ecosystem, which is so exquisitely rendered around a giant floating mountain as to draw gasps from first-time visitors.

Avatar: Flight of Passage

After a pre-flight briefing explaining how to pair with a banshee, you and 15 other cadets enter a chamber where you each strap into a vehicle, put on your 3D goggles and then take to the skies. This is one of the best and most immersive rides of any theme park, anywhere.

The jungle landscapes and seascapes feel completely real, and for added authenticity you can

PLANNING TIP

Pandora is beautiful during the day, but its otherworldly qualities really come out after sunset, when the bioluminescence makes you feel like you're on an alien moon. Which you are, of course.

Scan this QR code to help plan your trip to Pandora: The World of Avatar.

Pandora, bioluminescence

TAKE A BREAK
Satu'li Canteen (p77) serves customizable bowls with fresh, flavorful ingredients inspired by the world of Avatar in an immersive eco-friendly mess hall.

smell the faint must of the undergrowth and feel a splash on your face as you skim the surface of the water. It's all just another layer of magic that helps you immerse completely into the experience.

This is an incredibly popular ride: use Lightning Lane (157) or arrive early.

Na'vi River Journey

This slow meander through the bioluminescent world of Pandora is short on thrills but very high on beauty: for over 4½ minutes in a four-seater boat you drift past glowing flora and mysterious fauna. The ride climaxes in an encounter with the Na'vi Shaman of Songs, Pandora's life force, wonderfully rendered in audio-animatronics.

EXPERIENCES

Witness the Majestic Tree of Life

FAMILY FRIENDLY

MAP: 1 P70 C4

Discovery Island is the hub of the park, centered by the iconic **Tree of Life**. Standing at 145ft tall with over 300 animal carvings, the tree has been the park's symbol since Animal Kingdom's first opened in 1998.

Starting in winter 2025, the brand new *Zootopia: Better Zoo-gether* show, will take place inside the tree at the Tree of Life theater, featuring everyone's favorite cop-and-con duo, Judy Hopps and Nick Wilde. You can also hike the **Discovery Island Trails**, screne pathways that wind around the Tree of Life where you can observe a variety of animals, including flamingos, otters and tortoises, from convenient observation points. Interact with Mickey and Minnie Mouse dressed in their safari outfits at their exploration headquarters, **Adventurers Outpost**, a character meet-and-greet location.

A nightly show highlights the beauty and interconnectedness of nature, showcasing the diverse creatures carved into the tree.

Spot Wildlife on Kilimanjaro Safaris

FAMILY FRIENDLY

MAP: 2 P70 A2

Board an open-sided **safari vehicle** for a thrilling journey through the African savanna, pausing to observe zebras, lions, giraffes, alligators and more, all seemingly roaming free. Sometimes you'll have to wait to let an animal cross the road, and if you're lucky you'll see babies or some raucous activity. The informative guides provide fascinating insights into the wildlife and ecosystem, and you'll also see hippos, rhinos and other large mammals, giving the experience a real-life safari feel.

At 110 acres, the safari grounds are the largest attraction at any Disney theme park anywhere – the Magic Kingdom could just about fit inside this space. Though there are no animal barriers in sight, this is perhaps the safest safari on the planet. Disney revolutionized the world of animal habitats by creating large-scale spaces that make use of water features, moats and camouflaged fences to create natural enclosures. There's a carefully curated collection of flora as well, including millions of trees, grasses and shrubs from every continent on Earth except Antarctica.

Embark on a Starlight Safari

FAMILY FRIENDLY

If you've ever visited a zoo on a hot day and wondered where the animals are, then you probably know that they tend to be more active at night. And sure enough, as the sun sets at Disney's Animal Kingdom, the savanna awakens. On an **after-dark safari expedition**, you'll be able to catch all the wildlife in action. An open-sided safari vehicle whisks guests through lush scenery, and everyone is equipped with night-vision goggles to help you spot some of the more elusive creatures. This nighttime tour lasts approximately one hour and is available exclusively to guests eight years of age or older. Preregistration is required; prices start at $75 per person.

Visitors can also take advantage of the free night vision goggles at both Jambo House's Uzima Overlook (p76) and Kidani Village's **Kidani Rock Overlook**, where you can clearly see what the animals are up to after the sun goes down.

Find a Yeti on Expedition Everest ROLLER COASTER

MAP: 3 P70 **D4**

Expedition Everest is a tea-company-run train (er, roller coaster) that climbs 200ft from the mythical kingdom of Anandapur up to the snow-capped peak of the tallest summit in the world, Forbidden Mountain. The 25ft yeti lurking on the peak is the largest and most complex audio-animatronic figure at Disney.

Nearby, the self-guided **Maharajah Jungle Trek** introduces visitors to fascinating creatures, including acrobatic gibbons, a komodo dragon and tapirs. Mysterious Malayan flying foxes, among the largest known bats, hang from vines, while tigers regally await passersby from their dedicated temple.

Sing Along at the Festival of the Lion King SHOW

MAP: 4 P70 **B4**

Featuring acrobats, larger-than-life puppets, circus-inspired choreography and audience interaction, this **high-energy musical** is a visual and auditory delight that captures the spirit of the beloved Lion King. It doesn't follow the story line, but it does incorporate the characters and songs. Be prepared to belt out warthog, giraffe, lion and elephant noises!

BEAT THE HEAT

Though it's immersed in lush greenery, the Animal Kingdom is the hottest and most humid of all the Disney theme parks. To stay cool, aim for early morning arrival, bring a portable fan (available at most gift shops) or catch a show during the hottest part of the day. Take a cue from the animals who nap in the afternoon heat and return to your hotel in the afternoon – or enjoy the park after sunset. Stay hydrated by bringing a water bottle and refilling it at water stations around the park, and ride Kali River Rapids for a guaranteed big splash of cool water.

Expedition Everest
DISNEY ©

Cool off on the Kali River Rapids

WATER RIDE

MAP: 5 P70 **C4**

Wind through the rainforest, down gentle drops and past waterfalls on a 12-person circular raft on the Chakranadi River. Folks on the sidelines squirt water at the boats as they bounce down the **Kali River Rapids**, and it's a sure-fire guarantee that you'll get absolutely dripping-wet, wring-out-the-water-from-your-shirt soaked. If you'd rather be the soaker than the soakee, look for a small box with a green button on the bridge near the final stretch of Kali River Rapids. Press the button and the elephant statues spray water from their trunks and drench raft riders. Lock up phones and valuables in the free lockers.

Look for Silverbacks on the Gorilla Falls Exploration Trail

FAMILY FRIENDLY

MAP: 6 P70 **B3**

A troop of western lowland gorillas, the world's largest primates, calls Disney's Animal Kingdom home. Meet them on the **Gorilla Falls Exploration Trail**, a winding

GIRAFFE HABITATS

Standing up to 20ft in height, giraffes are the world's tallest land animal. They're also among the most fascinating, thanks to their long, stately necks and unique spotted patterns. Giraffes can usually be found browsing in the treetops at their Kilimanjaro Safaris habitat (p73). The **Uzima Overlook**, located at the Lodge's Jambo House, is home to another herd of giraffes. The concierge desk here offers the use of night-vision goggles for viewings between sundown and 9:30pm.

quarter-mile path where you'll encounter animals at every turn. Along the way, meerkats often mingle on their rocky perch and zebras can usually be found grazing on the savanna. Smaller animals live here, too, including the adorable Arabian spiny mouse, the naked mole-rat and the pancake tortoise.

But the primates that graze on their lush, hilly home are perhaps the most awesome of all. During your self-guided tour, observation stations make it easy to spot the gorillas and learn more about Disney's global conservation efforts to protect their habitats. It's hard to miss Gino, the park's resident 400lb silverback. One of the first gorillas in the world to allow his caretakers to perform a cardiac ultrasound without anesthesia, Gino helped launch a new method to protect his fellow gorillas from cardiac issues. He's a father, too, and can often be spotted roughhousing with his juvenile sons.

Learn about Conservation at Rafiki's Planet Watch

FAMILY FRIENDLY

MAP: 7 P70 **D1**

Join Rafiki, the wise and eccentric mandrill from *The Lion King*, to learn more about the circle of life at **Rafiki's Planet Watch**. Learn about animal care and conservation efforts, and watch veterinarians in action at Conservation Station. You can check out pet goats and lamas at Affection Section. To get here, take the **Wildlife Express Train**, a scenic train ride that takes you behind the scenes of Animal Kingdom, offering glimpses of animal care facilities and other backstage areas.

Best Places for...

See p70 for map of locations

$ Budget $$ Midrange $$$ Top End

Eating

Sit-Down Restaurants

Tiffins Restaurant $$$
8 B4
Experience dishes from around the globe in a beautifully themed environment. *11am-8pm*

Tusker House Restaurant $$$
9 B4
A colorful marketplace offering African-inspired buffet meals with character dining featuring Disney favorites. *7am-7pm*

Quick-Service Restaurants

Satu'li Canteen $$
10 B5
Create your own bowl at this Pandora restaurant. *11am-8pm*

Tamu Tamu Refreshments $$
11 B4
Grab refreshing treats ike Dole Whips and fresh fruit drinks in a colorful African-inspired marketplace. *10am-8pm*

Harambe Market $
12 B4
Savor African-inspired fare at this open-air spot. Lion King fans will want to save room for a Simba cupcake. *10:45am-3:15pm*

Mr Kamal's $

13 C4
The seasoned fries and chicken dumplings will hit the spot when you're in need of a quick snack. *10:30am-5pm*

Drinking

Bars

Thirsty River Bar
14 D4
Open-air bar offering specialty drinks and beers, along with a selection of refreshing frozen beverages. *11am-8pm*

Nomad Lounge

15 B4
Located on Discovery Island, this full-service bar features a wide range of beers, wines and specialty cocktails. *11am-8pm*

Dawa Bar
see 9 B4
Sidle up to the flat-roofed bar, order a sugarcane mojito and rest those Disney-weary bones. *11am-8pm*

Shopping

Souvenirs

Island Mercantile
16 C4
Features a wide range of Disney merchandise, all with an Animal Kingdom twist. *9am-9pm*

Mombasa Marketplace & Ziwani Traders
17 B4
Shop for African-inspired goods, much of which has been handcrafted by artisans. *8am-5:30pm*

Windtraders

18 B5
The main gift shop in Pandora, this is where you'll find Na'vi cultural items, *Avatar*-themed apparel and interactive toys. *7:45am-6:30pm*

See p84
for eating, drinking and shopping listings

Explore Disney Springs & Other Attractions

Explore beyond the four theme parks and discover the rest of what the Walt Disney World® Resort property has to offer. Disney Springs, which is Walt Disney World®'s vast – and free to enter – shopping, dining and entertainment district, keeps guests entertained for hours on end. Typhoon Lagoon and Blizzard Beach, the resort's two water parks, are always a blast, with their great combinations of thrill rides and laid-back lazy rivers. Want to invite a little friendly competition? Walt Disney World® Resort boasts two under-the-radar mini-golf courses with impeccable theming. Let's not forget to mention that the Disney hotels are jam-packed with activities that can take your Orlando trip to the next level. Boat parades, animal encounters, and life-size holiday gingerbread houses are just the beginning.

Getting Around

There are lots of options to get around the Walt Disney World® Resort property – from buses and boats to Skyliners, monorails, and Minnie Vans (p25). Don't be afraid to ask a cast member for help.

No matter how far these transportation options take you on the Walt Disney World® Resort property, you'll still want to be prepared to do quite a bit of walking once you reach your destination.

Disney Springs; Gazelle, Disney's Animal Kingdom Lodge (p82)

FROM LEFT: DAVSLENS - DAVSLENS.COM/SHUTTERSTOCK ©, OREN RAVID/ SHUTTERSTOCK ©

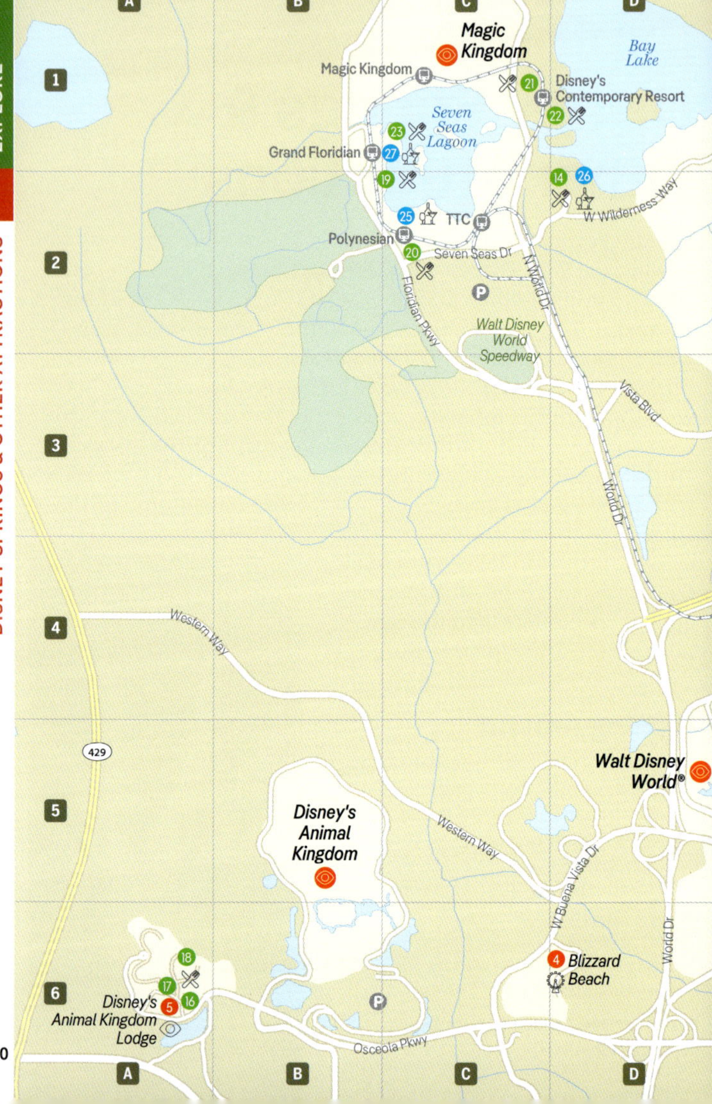
A
B
C
D
1
2
3
4
5
6
Magic Kingdom
Bay Lake
Magic Kingdom
21
Disney's Contemporary Resort
22
Seven Seas Lagoon
23
Grand Floridian
27
19
14
26
W Wilderness Way
25
TTC
Polynesian
20
Seven Seas Dr
N World Dr
Floridian Pkwy
Walt Disney World Speedway
Vista Blvd
World Dr
Western Way
429
Walt Disney World®
Disney's Animal Kingdom
Western Way
W Buena Vista Dr
18
17
16
Disney's Animal Kingdom Lodge
5
4
Blizzard Beach
World Dr
Osceola Pkwy

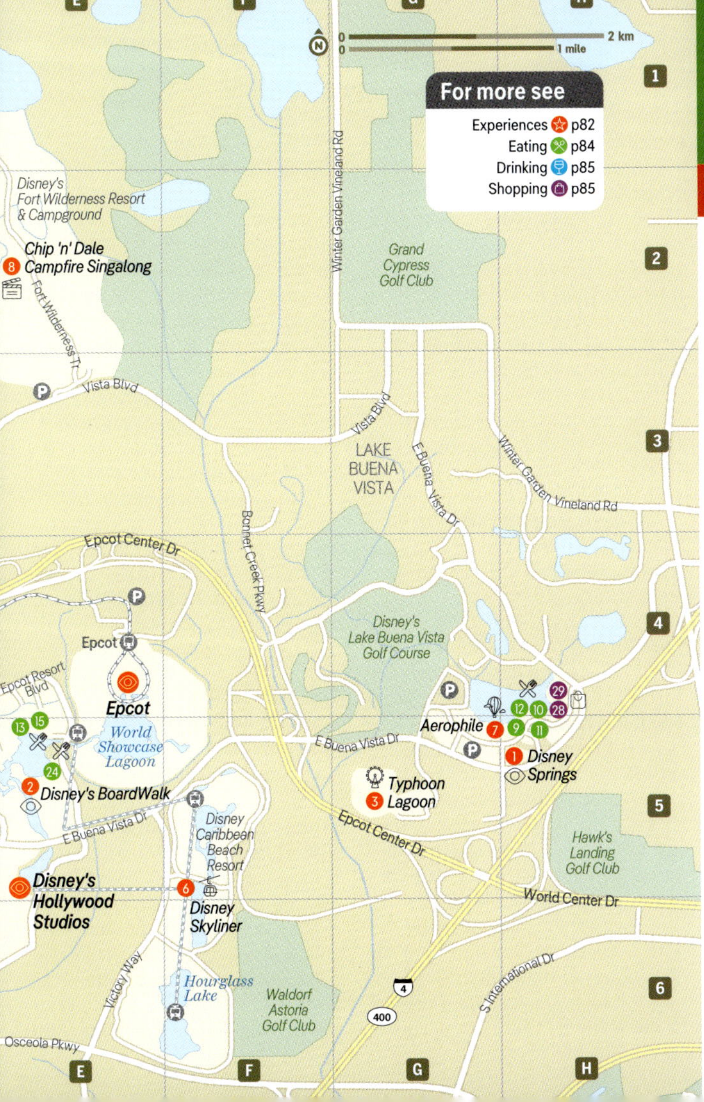
For more see
Experiences p82
Eating p84
Drinking p85
Shopping p85
0 2 km
0 1 mile
Disney's Fort Wilderness Resort & Campground
8 Chip 'n' Dale Campfire Singalong
Fort Wilderness Tr
Vista Blvd
Winter Garden Vineland Rd
Grand Cypress Golf Club
LAKE BUENA VISTA
E Buena Vista Dr
Bonnet Creek Pkwy
Epcot Center Dr
Epcot
Epcot Resort Blvd
Epcot
World Showcase Lagoon
2 Disney's BoardWalk
E Buena Vista Dr
Disney's Lake Buena Vista Golf Course
Aerophile 7
1 Disney Springs
Typhoon 3 Lagoon
Disney Caribbean Beach Resort
Disney's Hollywood Studios
6 Disney Skyliner
Hourglass Lake
Waldorf Astoria Golf Club
Victory Way
Hawk's Landing Golf Club
World Center Dr
S International Dr
Osceola Pkwy
4
400

EXPERIENCES

Shop & Dine at Disney Springs

SHOP

Disney Springs (MAP: 1 P81 **H5**) is primary entertainment district in Walt Disney World® – with shops, restaurants and bars, live music and a movie theater – stretches along the waterfront. You can take buses from Disney resorts to Disney Springs, and a few hotels offer boat transport to the area, but you cannot take Disney transport from here to any theme or water parks. Admission and parking is free.

For a one-stop shop, Disney Springs has the largest Disney character store in the country, with 12 massive rooms chock-a-block with everything you can imagine.

Disney's BoardWalk (MAP: 2 P81 **E5**) area across from Epcot is a smaller, fun-filled alternative to Disney Springs.

Putt through Fantasia Gardens & Fairways

MINI-GOLF

Just off Disney's BoardWalk, **Fantasia Gardens & Fairways** (see MAP: 2 P81 **E5**) offers a tranquil escape from the busy parks with its two 18-hole mini-golf courses. Putt through five whimsical scenes featuring Fantasia's tutu-clad hippos and dancing mushrooms. Beware of the marching broomsticks – they love to surprise passersby with a splash! Meanwhile, Fantasia Fairways was voted the longest and most challenging mini-golf course in the world by *Golf Digest*. This is a traditional golf course built on a miniature scale and is great for families with mini-golf experience.

Keep Cool at the Water Parks

WATER RIDE

Disney has two water parks: **Typhoon Lagoon** (MAP: 3 P81 **G5**; *adult/child $74/68*) and **Blizzard Beach** (MAP: 4 P80 **D6**; *adult/child $74/68*). Typhoon's white sandy beach, high-speed slides and the best wave pool in Orlando make this one of the best water parks in Florida. The most thrilling slide of them all is the **Crush 'n' Gusher** water coaster, but little ones will love floating along Castaway Creek.

Blizzard Beach is newer and themed as a melted ski resort, offering exciting water slides such as thrilling **Slush Gusher drop**, a lazy river and the **Summit Plummet**, a 12-story free-fall slide with speeds up to 55mph.

See Wandering Animals and African Art Collection

FAMILY-FRIENDLY

Inspired by the kraal, a traditional Southern African herding village, **Disney's Animal Kingdom Lodge** (MAP: 5 P80 **A6**) is surrounded by four lush savannas populated by over 200 animals and birds, including giraffes, impalas, bongos and gazelles. It's also home to the largest collection of African art outside the African continent. Even if you're not staying here, you can pop in to see the artwork. Over 4380 stunning museum-quality pieces showcase the many traditions of Africa, making this resort feel more like an art museum than a hotel. Don't miss the collection's revered 16' x 8' Igbo Ijele mask in the lobby.

Take to the Skies FAMILY FRIENDLY

In 2019, the free **Disney Skyliner** (MAP: 6 P81 **F5**) soared into the air over Walt Disney World®, adding an extra dash of pixie dust and a new transportation option. From a central terminus at Disney's Caribbean Beach Resort, this 6-mile state-of-the-art gondola travels at 11mph 60ft above the ground, connecting Disney's Hollywood Studios and Epcot to Disney's Art of Animation Resort, Disney's Pop Century Resort and Disney's Riviera Resort. Above the treetops, it's perhaps the most relaxing way to get around.

Go higher still on the **Aerophile** (MAP: 7 P81 **G5**; *adult/child $30/25*), a tethered hot-air balloon ride at Disney Springs. Floating 400ft above ground, it offers stunning panoramas of the entire resort.

Roast Marshmallows at the Chip 'n' Dale Campfire Singalong SHOW

MAP: 8 P81 **E2**

Located at Disney's Fort Wilderness Resort, this **family-friendly event** features a cozy campfire where guests can roast marshmallows and enjoy a lively singalong led by Chip and Dale (*free*). It's followed by a classic Disney movie under the stars, typically starting around 7pm. Don't forget to grab your s'mores kit from the **Chuckwagon Snack Bar** for the ultimate campfire experience.

Unwind at the Electrical Water Pageant SHOW

The **nightly parade** of illuminated floats on the Seven Seas Lagoon and Bay Lake features a colorful display of sea creatures and iconic Disney tunes, and it can be viewed from various waterfront resorts at around 9pm – the best spot being the shores of the Polynesian and Grand Floridian resorts. Make sure to get there early for a prime viewing spot and bring along a blanket for a cozy evening under the stars.

COLLECTIBLE SOUVENIRS

For just 51¢, **pressed pennies** are one of the most inexpensive souvenirs in all of Walt Disney World®. The My Disney Experience app provides a location map of pressed-coin machines: there are over 130 of them in Disney's Hollywood Studios alone! The machines take an ordinary penny and transform it into an oval-shaped, copper treasure embossed with a Disney character, attraction or unique logo. The available designs change constantly, making them highly collectible.

Best Places for...

See p80 for map of locations

$ Budget $$ Midrange $$$ Top End

Eating

Disney Springs

Chef Art Smith's Homecomin' $$
9 H5
Local celebrity chef shares his love of Southern comfort food, including fried chicken and moonshine cocktails. *11am-11pm*

T-Rex Cafe $$
10 H4
This dinosaur-themed restaurant offers a pre-historic dining adventure overseen by animatronic dinosaurs. *11am-11pm*

Frontera Cocina $$
11 H5
Chef Rick Bayless serves classic Mexican favorites like tacos al pastor (marinated pork) and signature guacamole and chips. Fun margarita-filled happy hours, too. *11am-11pm*

Boathouse $$
12 H4
A nautical-themed restaurant that offers waterfront dining with a menu featuring fresh seafood, steaks and the chance to take a ride in an Amphicar. *11am-11pm*

Disney Resorts

Yachtsman Steakhouse $$$
13 E5
This elegant New England style steakhouse at Disney's Yacht Club Resort specializes in premium steaks, fresh seafood, and savory side dishes. *5-9:30pm*

Whispering Canyon Cafe $$
14 D2
Located in Disney's Wilderness Lodge, this Western-themed restaurant offers hearty American cuisine like barbecue pulled pork, ribs, and chicken in a lively atmosphere. *7:30am-10pm*

Beaches and Cream Soda Shop $$
15 E5
This retro soda fountain at Disney's Beach Club Resort serves classic American favorites like burgers, fries and ice cream while immersing guests in nostalgia. *11am-11pm*

Boma $$$
16 A6
In Disney's Animal Kingdom Lodge, Boma offers an all-you-can-eat buffet featuring African-inspired dishes and American classics in a grand dining room that evokes an African marketplace. *7:30-11:30am & 5-9:30pm*

Sanaa $$
17 A6
At Disney's Kidani Village, Sanaa serves African and Indian-inspired cuisine with views of savanna animals and an extensive wine list featuring stellar South African wines. *7:30am-9:30pm*

Jiko $$$
18 A6
Located at Disney's Animal Kingdom Lodge, Jiko offers a unique blend of African, Mediterranean and Indian cuisines with signature dishes like grilled wild-boar tenderloin and African spice-infused flatbreads. *5-9:30pm*

Victoria & Albert's $$$
 19 C2
Perhaps the finest restaurant in all of Walt Disney World, this award-winning restaurant at Disney's Grand Floridian Resort & Spa features gourmet dining with a sophisticated, romantic ambience. *5:30-8pm Tue-Sat*

'Ohana $$$
20 C2
At Disney's Polynesian Village Resort, 'Ohana offers a family-style feast with South Pacific flavors and a fun, laid-back atmosphere. *7:30am-noon & 3:30-10pm*

California Grill $$$
 21 C1
Perched atop Disney's Contemporary Resort, this elegant restaurant emphasizes fresh, sustainable ingredients. Floor-to-ceiling windows means it's great for fireworks. *5-10pm*

Chef Mickey's $$$
 22 D1
Dine with the best mouses in the world, Mickey and Minnie, as you dig into a buffet featuring all the kid-friendly fare you crave. At Disney's Contemporary Resort. *7:30am-12:30pm & 5-9:30pm*

Narcoossee's $$$
 23 C1
Upscale yet casual, with nautical decor, this waterfront restaurant at Disney's Grand Floridian Resort & Spa specializes in fresh seafood and steaks. Start with a champagne toast as you enjoy the panoramic views of the Seven Seas Lagoon. *5-9:30pm*

Flying Fish $$$
 24 E5
Located on Disney's BoardWalk, seafood delights fly onto plates in this fun, open kitchen dining spot. *5-9:30pm*

Drinking

Bars

Trader Sam's Grog Grotto & Tiki Bar
 25 C2
Located at Disney's Polynesian Village Resort, this whimsical tiki bar features exotic cocktails, hidden Mickeys and a South Seas vibe. *3pm-midnight*

Geyser Point Bar & Grill
 26 D2
An outdoor bar at Disney's Wilderness Lodge with stunning views of the resort's geyser and a variety of craft beers. *11am-11pm*

Enchanted Rose Lounge
 27 C1
An upscale cocktail bar at Disney's Grand Floridian Resort that immerses guests in a romantic *Beauty and the Beast* atmosphere. *3:30-11pm*

Shopping

Souvenirs

World of Disney
28 H4
Don't miss the chance to snag that perfect souvenir for the Disney fans in your life at the world's largest Disney store. *10am-11pm*

Lego Imagination Center
see 28 H4
Let your creativity run wild at this vibrant store featuring interactive displays, a Pick-A-Brick wall and a creative workshop. *10am-11pm*

Marketplace Co-op
 29 H4
Explore this eclectic marketplace for artisanal goods and Disney-themed products. *10am-11pm*

UNIVERS

Explore Universal, Orlando & Beyond

Worth a Trip

Universal Studios (p93)
UNIVERSAL ORLANDO RESORT ©

★ OVERVIEW

Universal Orlando Resort

Universal Orlando Resort, one of the premier theme-park destinations in the world, is where Hollywood comes to life. With four parks, one shopping and dining district, and a slew of hotels, there's a whole lot to explore in this movie-inspired world.

MAP: **P90**

PLANNING TIP
Try to get early park admission at Universal Orlando Resort, either by staying at a resort hotel or by booking a specific vacation package. This is a great way to beat the lines on the best rides.

Download the Universal Orlando Resort app to make your visit a breeze.

The Universal Theme Parks

As of 2025, there are three Universal Orlando Resort theme parks: ❶ **Universal Studios** (p93), ❷ **Islands of Adventure** (p101) and ❸ **Universal Epic Universe** (p114), each with its own flair. Cinema fans will love Universal Studios in particular, with rides like E.T. Adventure and shops like the Film Vault. Islands of Adventure tends to be a favorite for those looking for a more classic theme-park experience. Character experiences, hidden foodie delights and next-level thrill rides are just the beginning. Opened in 2025, brand-new Epic Universe is the latest playground is filled with themed lands, rides and restaurants that are guaranteed to be crowd favorites, from the Viking-inspired thrills in How to Train Your Dragon to the interactive games of Super Nintendo World.

The Water Park: Volcano Bay

In addition to the three theme parks, Universal Orlando Resort also has a water park, and they've done it well. During your visit to ❹ **Volcano Bay** (p112), you'll be transported to an island oasis, home to the 200ft Krakatau Volcano. With 19 rides and attractions, you can discover new thrills,

Universal Helios Grand Hotel, Universal Epic Universe (p114)

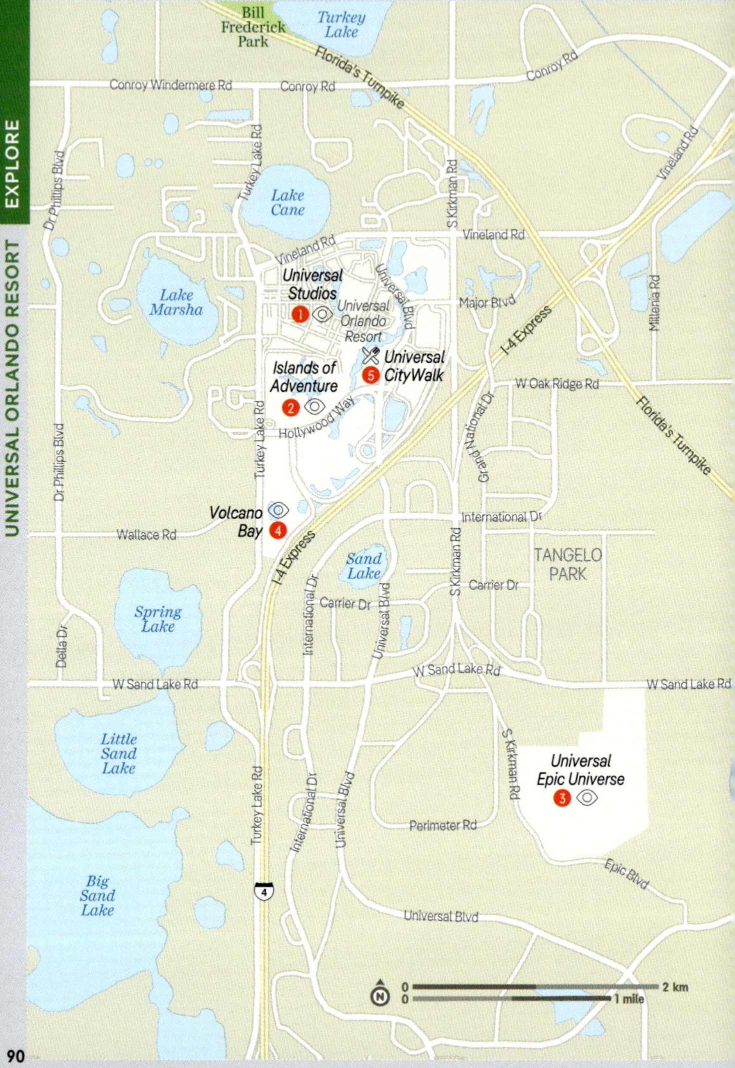
Bill Frederick Park
Turkey Lake
Florida's Turnpike
Conroy Windermere Rd
Conroy Rd
Conroy Rd
Dr Phillips Blvd
Turkey Lake Rd
Lake Cane
S Kirkman Rd
Vineland Rd
Vineland Rd
Vineland Rd
Lake Marsha
Universal Studios
1
Universal Orlando Resort
Universal Blvd
Major Blvd
Millenia Rd
I-4 Express
Islands of Adventure
2
Universal CityWalk
5
W Oak Ridge Rd
Hollywood Way
Grand National Dr
Florida's Turnpike
Turkey Lake Rd
Dr Phillips Blvd
Volcano Bay
4
International Dr
Wallace Rd
I-4 Express
Sand Lake
TANGELO PARK
S Kirkman Rd
Carrier Dr
Carrier Dr
International Dr
Universal Blvd
Spring Lake
Delta Dr
W Sand Lake Rd
W Sand Lake Rd
W Sand Lake Rd
Little Sand Lake
S Kirkman Rd
Universal Epic Universe
3
Turkey Lake Rd
International Dr
Universal Blvd
Perimeter Rd
Epic Blvd
4
Big Sand Lake
Universal Blvd
N
0
2 km
0
1 mile

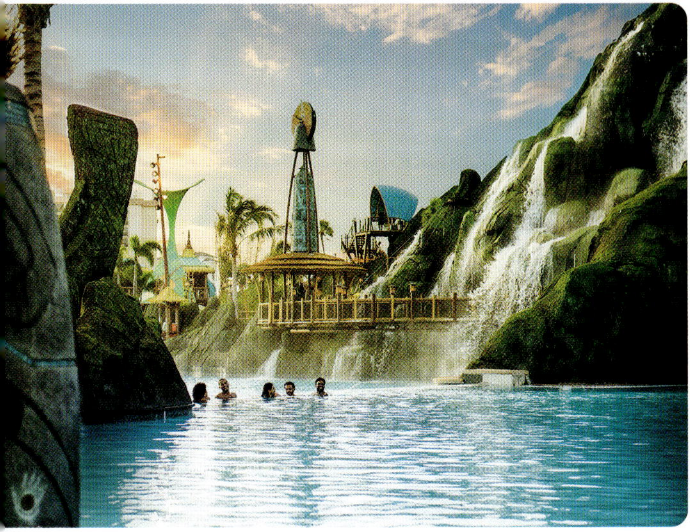

Volcano Bay (p112)

give your little ones the times of their lives at the kid-friendly splash zones or cool off on the chill rides and attractions.

Dining & Shopping at Universal CityWalk

Usually labeled as a shopping district, 5 **Universal CityWalk** (p109) is more of a restaurant hot spot than anything else, with foodie gems like Cowfish Sushi Burger Bar and the sweet Toothsome Chocolate Emporium & Savory Feast Kitchen. Scattered amid the many eateries, you'll find a couple of activities that are worth your time as well – break out of the complex, movie-inspired puzzle rooms at Universal Great Movie Escape or embrace a bit of friendly competition at Hollywood Drive-In Golf. You'll pass through CityWalk on your way to Universal Studios and Islands of Adventure, so be sure to dedicate some time to exploring this cool area.

TAKE A BREAK

Enjoy the lesser-known parts of Universal Orlando. When staying at a Universal Signature Collection resort, for example, you can take advantage of the pool-hopping perk.

See p99 for eating, drinking and shopping listings

Explore
Universal Studios

Universal Studios is for movie lovers, offering visitors a behind-the-scenes glimpse into blockbuster film and TV production. None other than legendary director Steven Spielberg served as a creative consultant for Universal Studios Orlando way back in 1986 – four years before the park officially opened to the public.

Now, it's your chance to step into the leading movie role, casting spells with your wand like Harry Potter, transforming yourself into a lovable Despicable Me minion and fighting aliens alongside the Men in Black. Across eight different lands, you'll have countless opportunities to experience the magic of cinema firsthand.

Getting Around

On Foot

There's no transportation inside Universal Studios, so buy a good pair of shoes and get ready to walk.

Wheelchairs & Strollers

Rent strollers, wheelchairs and electric convenience vehicles (ECVs) at the entrance to the park.

Other Parks

If you're going to the Islands of Adventure, you can take the Hogwarts Express or go on foot via Universal CityWalk. And if you're headed to Universal Epic Universe, there will likely be buses to take you between parks.

The Wizarding World of Harry Potter: Diagon Alley

THE BEST

THRILL RIDE Revenge of the Mummy (p98)

CAPTIVATING SHOW The Bourne Stuntacular (p97)

DESSERT STOP Florean Fortescue's Ice Cream Parlor (p99)

HIDDEN HOTSPOT Knockturn Alley (p95)

FILM STORE The Film Vault (p99)

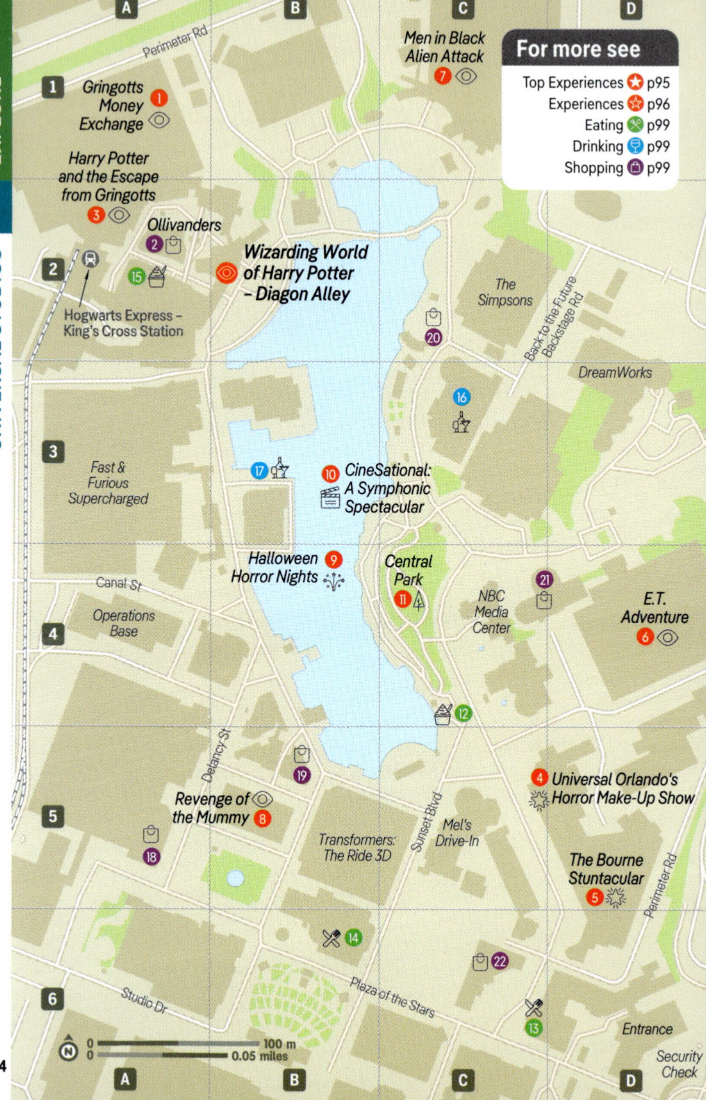

For more see
Top Experiences p95
Experiences p96
Eating p99
Drinking p99
Shopping p99
Perimeter Rd
Gringotts Money Exchange 1
Harry Potter and the Escape from Gringotts 3
Ollivanders 2
Hogwarts Express – King's Cross Station
15
Wizarding World of Harry Potter – Diagon Alley
Men in Black Alien Attack 7
The Simpsons
Back to the Future Backstage Rd
20
DreamWorks
16
17
CineSational: A Symphonic Spectacular 10
Fast & Furious Supercharged
Halloween Horror Nights 9
Central Park 11
NBC Media Center
21
E.T. Adventure 6
Canal St
Operations Base
12
Delancy St
19
4 Universal Orlando's Horror Make-Up Show
Revenge of the Mummy 8
18
Transformers: The Ride 3D
Sunset Blvd
Mel's Drive-In
The Bourne Stuntacular 5
Perimeter Rd
14
22
Plaza of the Stars
Studio Dr
13
Entrance
Security Check
100 m
0.05 miles

★ TOP EXPERIENCE

Wizarding World of Harry Potter – Diagon Alley

Aspiring Harry Potter wizards should pick up an interactive wand at Ollivanders, after which you'll be able to cast dozens of spells at various hidden locations around the **Wizarding World of Harry Potter – Diagon Alley** in Universal Studios and Hogsmeade (p108) in Islands of Adventure, making objects levitate, revealing hidden messages and more.
MAP: **B2**

The Wand Chooses the Wizard

First thing's first: you'll need a wand to start casting spells. There are a number of places to pick one up – both inside and outside of the Wizarding World of Harry Potter – but, as Hagrid likes to put it, Ollivanders (p96) is 'the only place for wands.' There, shop employees will help the right wand find you. Note that not all wands are interactive wands.

Master Magic: Using Your Wand

Wand in hand, wander the streets of Diagon Alley, searching for designated interactive wand locations. Look for gold medallions on the ground, which show you the wand movement and size to cast the spell. Make marionettes dance outside of **Pilliwinkle's Playthings** with the Tarantallegra spell or repair a suit of armor at **Brown E Wright's blacksmith shop** with the Reparo spell – all with just a couple of quick flicks of the wrist. Don't forget to venture into **Knockturn Alley**, where five interactive wand spots are hidden away in the dark, less busy corridors. In total, there are 17 interactive wand spots in Diagon Alley and Knockturn Alley, along with another nine in Hogsmeade.

PLANNING TIP
Bring your wand map to the tucked-away Knockturn Alley. There, below the 'Noggin and Bonce' sign, you'll find a black light that will reveal secret interactive wand spots.

Scan this QR code for a complete list of interactive wand spots.

EXPERIENCES

Watch a Dragon Breathe Fire
SHOW

MAP: 1 P94 A1

The Ukrainian Ironbelly dragon atop **Gringotts Money Exchange** puts on a fire-breathing show every 15 minutes or so. When you hear a low rumble, get ready for the dragon to release a flame hot enough to be felt three stories below.

Hitch a Ride on the Hogwart's Express
RIDE

Hop aboard the **Hogwarts Express** for a train ride filled with wizardry. While marketed as a ride, it's more of a fun form of transportation than anything else. On the ride from Universal Studios to Islands of Adventure – or really, between London and Hogsmeade – you'll feel magic seep into the air. Harry, Ron and Hermoine make brief appearances – and so does one less-than-friendly creature. Hopefully you won't get too spooked!

Be sure to catch the Hogwarts Express both ways, as the journey – and its magical surprises – are different each way.

In order to ride on the Hogwarts Express, you'll need a park-to-park ticket that grants you access to both Islands of Adventure (p101) and Universal Studios on the same day.

Change Muggle Cash at the Gringotts Money Exchange
FAMILY FRIENDLY

Immerse yourself in the wizarding world by exchanging your muggle money for Gringotts bank notes at **Gringotts Money Exchange** (*see* 1). You'll be greeted by a mischievous goblin who will guide you through this magical transaction. Keep the Harry Potter bank notes as a souvenir or spend them around the Wizarding World.

Find Your Wand at Ollivander's
SHOW

MAP: 2 P94 A2

As every Potterhead knows, the wand chooses the wizard. And at **Ollivanders**, this tale can become a reality. Throughout the day, Ollivanders runs a show for about 25 people. Of those 25, one is selected to be the star, the one that the perfect fit of a wand will deign to choose – a magical memory for any lucky Harry Potter fan.

If you aren't chosen, you can still peruse the wand selection at Ollivanders, and friendly cast members will help match you with the wand that best suits your personality.

IN-PARK SHIPPING

Want to purchase merch in the parks but don't want to lug it around? Send it to the Universal Studios Store at CityWalk (p110) and pick up your goodies on the way out of the parks. If you're staying at a Universal Studios Resort hotel, your items can be delivered directly to your room.

Survive Voldemort in the Escape from Gringotts

THRILL RIDE

MAP: 3 P94 **A2**

The line through lavish Gringotts Money Exchange, staffed by a cast of animatronic goblins, is almost as much of a highlight as the **Harry Potter and the Escape from Gringotts** ride itself. But soon enough, you'll be hurtling underground through the secret Gringotts vaults, where you'll face off with some of Harry Potter's most infamous villains: Bellatrix Lestrange and Voldemort. Luckily, Harry, Ron, Hermione and the Ironbelly dragon are on your side.

Experience Movie Magic at the Horror Make-Up Show

SHOW

MAP: 4 P94 **C5**

To learn all about how makeup artists create film monsters, catch the lively and very funny 25-minute **Horror Make-Up Show**, which pulls back the bandages to reveal the secrets behind fake wounds, severed limbs and movie gore.

Be Stunned by Stunts at the Bourne Stuntacular

SHOW

MAP: 5 P94 **D5**

An action-packed experience filled with stunts, pyrotechnics and a top-notch storyline, this Jason Bourne–inspired show will have you at the edge of your seat. Weirdly enough, if there happens to be a glitch during the show, it will only add to the **Bourne Stuntacular** experience, with a producer coming out to give you some more behind-the-scenes info on the magic of stagecraft.

Embrace Nostalgia on the E.T. Adventure

FAMILY FRIENDLY

MAP: 6 P94 **D4**

A classic Universal ride, **E.T. Adventure** is one for the nostalgia seekers. Jump aboard the flying bicycle and help the homesick alien save the planet, all the while dodging the baddies.

Save the World on Men in Black Alien Attack

THRILL RIDE

MAP: 7 P94 **B5**

Race through downtown Manhattan, blasting silly-looking aliens with powerful lasers and racking up well-earned points on this 3D video-game-esque ride.

Bonus: **Men in Black Alien Attack** is one of several rides that offers secret, free behind-the-scenes tours and Men in Black's is widely regarded as the best of the bunch. You'll get to wander the alien office, snap a few pictures with aliens, sign the log book, and sit in the ever-iconic – and supremely uncomfortable – white chairs. To enjoy this free tour, ask a Men in Black cast member. However, tours are not always available. The cast member must receive manager approval, and the ride must be adequately staffed and not too busy. If these conditions aren't met, you may be turned away.

Scream Your Lungs Out on Revenge of the Mummy

ROLLER COASTER

MAP: 8 P94 B5

Dive deep into ancient Egyptian catacombs on **Revenge of the Mummy**. Inspired by the 1932 horror film, *The Mummy*, this ride comes with as many special effects and scares as twists and turns. Be sure to avoid the wrath of the mummy, Imhotep!

Get Spooked during Halloween Horror Nights

SPECIAL EVENT

MAP: 9 P94 B4

On the nights leading up to Halloween, Universal Studios is decked out in all its horrifying glory. Officially known as **Halloween Horror Nights** (*admission from $83*), this isn't your average haunted house event. The 10 haunted houses and five scare zones are sure to get your heart racing, thanks to the talented actors, elaborate sets and terrifying special effects that will chill you to the bone.

Round Out Your Day with CineSational

SHOW

Stick around the park until late to experience the magic of a live Universal Resort night show. **CineSational: A Symphonic Spectacular** (MAP: 10 P94 B3) features iconic movie scores, dancing water fountains, and breathtaking fireworks. Head to the middle of **Central Park** (MAP: 11 P94 C4) to snag the best seats in the house!

Best Places for...

$ Budget $$ Midrange $$$ Top End

Eating

Quick-Service Restaurants

Central Park Crepes $
12 C4
A little kiosk with sweet and savory crepes that are some of the best bites in the park. *11am-close*

TODAY Cafe $
13 C6
The grab-and-go pastries and sandwiches at this cafe are ideal if you're looking for fresh and light bites. *9am-close*

Illumination's Minions Cafe $

14 B6
A surprising highlight, with dishes like Evil Minion Totchos, which are equal parts tasty and creative. *11am-close*

Sweet Treats

Florean Fortescue's Ice Cream Parlor $
15 A2
This Harry Potter–inspired ice-cream shop boasts fun flavors like clotted cream and the ever-classic butterbeer. *9am-close*

Drinking

Themed Drinks

Moe's Tavern

16 C3
Try Duff, Duff Lite and Duff Dry, made by the Florida Beer Company. Don't miss the non-alcoholic Flaming Moe's. *11am-close*

Chez Alcatraz

17 B3
The themed specialty cocktails here can't be beat. Order Ocean Attack for a special surprise with your drink. *11am-close*

Shopping

Universal Must-Sees

Universal Tribute Store
18 A5
A seasonal can't-miss pop-up with impeccable theming and the coolest merch – usually found in the New York or Hollywood sections. *hours vary*

The Film Vault

19 B5
A classic movie buff's dream, the Film Vault has everything from E.T. plushies to Ghostbusters figurines to the occasional signed movie poster. *hours vary*

Character-Inspired Shops

Kwik-E-Mart

20 C2
Fans of the Simpsons can find an extraordinary array of show-inspired goods. *9am-9pm*

SpongeBob StorePants
21 C4
If you're a fan of Bikini Bottom, this store has all the themed merch you could ever imagine. *9am-9pm*

Hello Kitty Store
22 C6
Hello Kitty mugs, backpacks, plushies and desserts await at this adorable shop. *9am-9pm*

See p109
for eating,
drinking and
shopping
listings

Explore
Islands of Adventure

Explore the eight-island archipelago inhabited by a cast of characters, including Hello Kitty, the Grinch, Wolverine and the Cat in the Hat, among others. Despite their (relatively) peaceful coexistence, villains lurk – and you are tasked with saving the day. At Marvel Super Hero Island, help Spider-Man protect the Statue of Liberty. At Jurassic Park, fight off velociraptors left and right. Take a break at the kid-friendly Seuss Landing or Toon Lagoon. And don't miss the most popular island around, the Wizarding World of Harry Potter: Hogsmeade, where three thrilling rides and an abundance of butterbeer will send you into the pages of the iconic series.

Getting Around

On Foot

Like Universal Studios, you'll need to walk everywhere in the Islands of Adventure.

Wheelchairs & Strollers

Rent strollers, wheelchairs and electric convenience vehicles (ECVs) at the entrance to the park.

Other Parks

If you're going to Universal Studios, you can either take the Hogwarts Express (p107) or go on foot via Universal CityWalk (p110). If you're going to Universal Epic Universe, there will likely be buses to take you between the parks.

THE BEST

THRILL RIDE Jurassic World VelociCoaster (p105)

BURGER JOINT Wimpy's (p109)

'ANIMAL' ENCOUNTER Jurassic Park Discovery Center (p107)

COCKTAIL BAR Hog's Head Pub (p109)

SIT-DOWN RESTAURANT Mythos Restaurant (p109)

Jurassic World VelociCoaster (p105)
UNIVERSAL ORLANDO RESORT ©

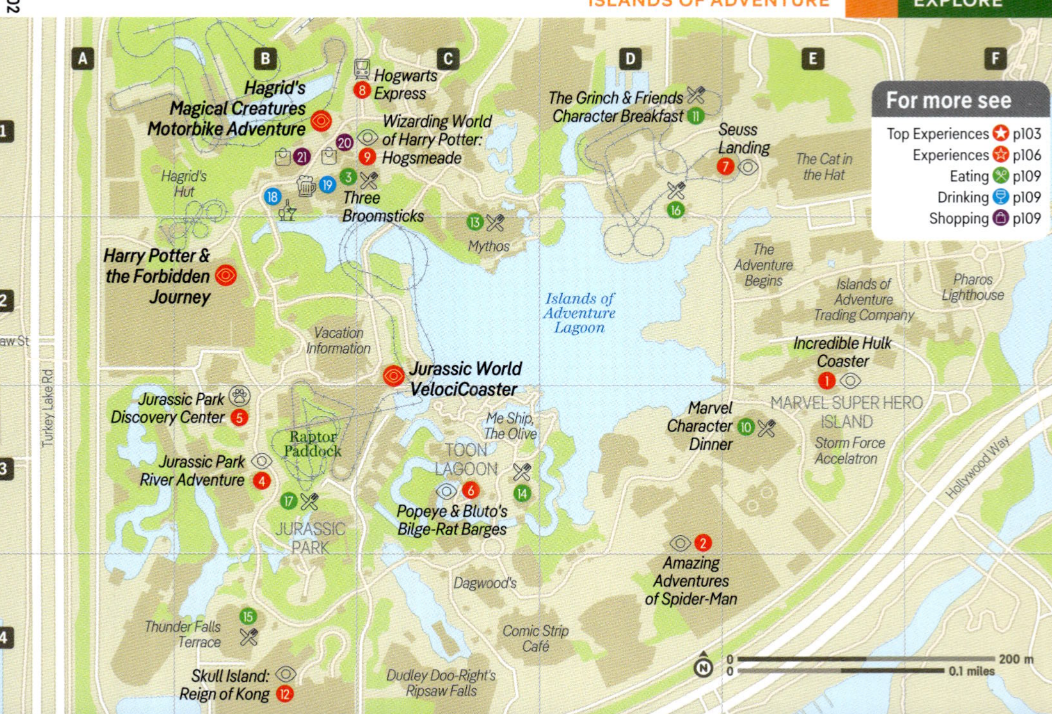
For more see
Top Experiences p103
Experiences p106
Eating p109
Drinking p109
Shopping p109
Hagrid's Magical Creatures Motorbike Adventure
Hogwarts Express
Wizarding World of Harry Potter: Hogsmeade
Hagrid's Hut
Three Broomsticks
Mythos
Harry Potter & the Forbidden Journey
Vacation Information
Jurassic World VelociCoaster
Jurassic Park Discovery Center
Raptor Paddock
Jurassic Park River Adventure
JURASSIC PARK
Me Ship, The Olive
TOON LAGOON
Popeye & Bluto's Bilge-Rat Barges
Dagwood's
Thunder Falls Terrace
Comic Strip Café
Skull Island: Reign of Kong
Dudley Do-Right's Ripsaw Falls
The Grinch & Friends Character Breakfast
Seuss Landing
The Cat in the Hat
Islands of Adventure Lagoon
The Adventure Begins
Islands of Adventure Trading Company
Pharos Lighthouse
Incredible Hulk Coaster
MARVEL SUPER HERO ISLAND
Marvel Character Dinner
Storm Force Accelatron
Amazing Adventures of Spider-Man
Hollywood Way
Turkey Lake Rd
Paw St
0 200 m
0 0.1 miles

★ TOP EXPERIENCE

Hagrid's Magical Creatures Motorbike Adventure

Hagrid's Magical Creatures Motorbike Adventure is truly a one-of-a-kind ride. Sometimes called a 'story coaster,' it's a roller coaster that provides thrills and an exceptional plot. Make sure to ride it again at night for a completely different experience.

MAP: **B1**

The Story

As the name of the ride implies, Hagrid himself will be your guide on this storybook adventure, as he takes you around the Forbidden Forest. And as the gamekeeper and professor of Care of Magical Creatures, he's got a whole lot of enchanted beasts for you to come face-to-face with, including blast-ended skrewts, Cornish pixies, and Fluffy, the three-headed dog. With Hagrid at the helm, it's inevitable that things won't go all that smoothly – but don't worry, he'll get them fixed up in a jiffy!

The Ride

Hop onboard your designated motorbike or sidecar. (If you're a little hesitant to ride, the sidecar may be the better option.) This launch coaster will, well, launch you forward at seven different points in the ride, after slowing down to hear a part of the story. Even though the stops and starts are frequent, don't expect the speeds to be moderate. Hagrid's tops out at 50mph! It's safe to say that you'll enjoy the full three-minute journey, which spans nearly a mile in length.

PLANNING TIP

If you have early access to the park, head straight to Hagrid's. It's likely the only time the wait will be under an hour – or even two – the entire day.

Scan this QR code for information on height requirements, accessibility and more.

★ TOP EXPERIENCE

Harry Potter & the Forbidden Journey

Climb aboard a broomstick and race through Hogwarts on this beloved Wizarding World of Harry Potter ride. A combination of 3D screens and intricate props bring this magical experience to life.

MAP: P102 **B2**

PLANNING TIP
You'll need to store your belongings in a locker (free) for this one. And while you're not required to put your phone away, it is recommended. You'll be flipped and twirled every which way!

Scan this QR code for information on height requirements, accessibility and more.

Wander Through Hogwarts

While waiting in line, you'll wander through dimly lit Hogwarts. Keep an eye for all sorts of Harry Potter memorabilia, from griffin statues to a copy of *The Daily Prophet* to the ever-revered Sorting Hat. You'll even get a glimpse of a Dark Arts classroom – complete with evil spells written on a chalkboard and a quick appearance by Harry, Hermione and Ron.

Strap in for a Topsy-Turvy Experience

While there are many unique modes of transportation in Universal Orlando Resort – trains (p107), motorcycles (p103), and water rafts (p107) – the Forbidden Journey's broomstick is the nimblest of all, taking you on unexpected twists and turns. Along the way, you'll cross paths with whomping willows and giant spiders, dragons and dementors. You'll even get to jump into a Quidditch match for a few seconds! It includes many highlights from the Harry Potter series, all wrapped up in one experience.

Note that Harry Potter and the Forbidden Journey is known to induce motion sickness. If you find yourself getting a little nauseous, try to stare at your feet to lessen the vertigo.

★ TOP EXPERIENCE

Jurassic World VelociCoaster

Ready for the thrill of your life? Reaching up to 70mph and zipping through four inversions, the **Jurassic World VelociCoaster** is arguably the most adrenaline-pumping ride in the entire Universal Orlando Resort area.

MAP: P102 **C3**

Meet the Raptors

While waiting in line for the VelociCoaster, you'll come across quite a few *Jurassic Park* and *Jurassic World* surprises. And just before you begin the ride experience, you get to walk through the stables, where muzzled raptors stare you down.

Get Ready for a Wild Ride

The ride experience begins with a welcome video from Owen Grady and Claire Dearing of *Jurassic World*. While Grady seems hesitant to combine a zooming roller coaster with live dinosaurs, you'll be ushered off and strapped in – with a single lap bar, no less – before you know it. And in less than three seconds, you'll be racing along at 70mph, taking on four different inversions and getting a whopping 12 seconds of air time, all while dodging velociraptors left and right.

The Secret Behind-the-Scenes Tour

Want to take an even deeper dive into the VelociCoaster? This ride has a secret behind-the-scenes tour, held at the discretion of the cast members. Officially called the **Velocicoaster Paddock Tour**, this 20-minute experience is filled with fun facts – and even a quick visit to the Mosasaurus.

PLANNING TIP

The VelociCoaster is known for its intense g-force, which can lead to brief blackout moments for some riders. To minimize this risk, ask for Row 6 for the mildest experience and stay hydrated.

Scan this QR code for information on height requirements, accessibility and more.

EXPERIENCES

Turn Green on the Incredible Hulk Coaster

ROLLER COASTER

MAP: 1 P102 **E2**

So, you've decided to take part in Dr Bruce Banner's latest research experiment? Bold move. When things go awry, your newly received powers are uncontrolled. Blast off at 67mph on the **Incredible Hulk Coaster** before embarking on a series of twists and turns that'll have your head spinning. The g-force is strong on this one.

Battle the Bad Guys on the Amazing Adventures of Spider-Man

IMMERSIVE RIDE

MAP: 2 P102 **D3**

One of the best simulator 4D rides in the park, the high-def, high-tech **Amazing Adventures of Spider-Man** pits you against some of Spider-Man's deadliest enemies while coursing through the streets of New York. You'll feel every bump, every blast of heat and a splash of water from Hydro-Man, but Spidey himself will always have your back.

Sample Butterbeer in the Wizarding World of Harry Potter

EAT & DRINK

MAP: 3 P102 **B1**

A once-fictitious beverage, **butterbeer** is now the signature drink of the Wizarding World of Harry Potter. There are half-a-dozen variations of this (very) sweet, butterscotch-esque beverage scattered throughout the Wizarding World in all three Universal Orlando Resort theme parks.

First, there are the drinkable classics: cold, frozen and hot butterbeer. These can be found at almost every food or drink stop in Harry Potter land. You'll have to make an effort to try the remaining three butterbeer sweets. Honeydukes Candy Shop (p109) is the only place to find butterbeer fudge in Hogsmeade, and the same goes for **Three Broomsticks** with potted butterbeer. While you can find butterbeer ice cream at Three Broomsticks as well, take the Hogwarts Express (p107) to Diagon Alley for the best version of this treat.

Meet the Dinos on the Jurassic Park River Adventure

WATER RIDE

MAP: 4 P102 **B3**

The **Jurassic Park River Adventure** journey starts innocuously enough: you float past friendly vegetarian dinosaurs, and all seems well and good until those grass-munchin' friends are replaced by the reptiles of your nightmares. To escape the looming teeth of the giant T-Rex, you plunge 85ft to the water below!

Since you can get a little wet on this Jurassic Park ride, there are lockers available for rent. Unfortunately, since you can technically bring your gear on this ride (it'll just get wet), it costs $5 per small locker and $6 per large locker, with additional fees after 90 minutes.

Name a Baby Velociraptor at the Jurassic Park Discovery Center

FAMILY FRIENDLY

MAP: 5 P102 B3

Can you imagine getting to see a baby velociraptor hatch right before your eyes? Through the magic of 'bioengineering' (and puppetry), those dreams can become a reality at the **Jurassic Park Discovery Center**. This unscheduled event takes place every 40 minutes or so, so you won't have to stick around too long. If you're lucky enough to be chosen to name the baby raptor, you'll receive a birth certificate with both your name and the baby's name, and you can come check on your growing raptor whenever you'd like.

Get Soaked on Popeye & Bluto's Bilge-Rat Barges

WATER RIDE

MAP: 6 P102 C3

Work with spinach-eating Popeye to rescue Olive Oyl from Bluto – and an 18ft octopus! This **white-water rafting ride** is brilliant fun for the whole family, but be prepared to get very, very wet.

Soar above Seuss Landing

FAMILY FRIENDLY

MAP: 7 P102 E1

Bring the pages of a Dr Seuss story to life in **Seuss Landing**. While all rides in this whimsical land are geared to children, **The High in the Sky Trolley Train Ride** is arguably the best of the bunch. Once settled into the playfully designed four-person carts, enjoy a retelling of a 1953 Dr Seuss favorite, **The Sneetches and Other Stories**. From here, take in a bird's-eye view of Seuss Land and beyond. It's even more spectacular at night and during the holidays.

Hitch a Ride on the Hogwarts Express

FAMILY FRIENDLY

MAP: 8 P102 C1

The **Hogwarts Express** is more of a next-level form of transportation than a ride, but it's certainly worth your time (assuming the wait is a reasonable 20 minutes or less). While the train cars can get quite stuffy in the summer, you'll see landscapes from Harry Potter passing right outside your window

EXPRESS PASSES: YAY OR NAY?

Universal Orlando Resort offers **Express Passes** to skip most standard ride lines. Prices vary depending on the day and the Express Pass tier, but expect to pay hundreds per person. While expensive, these add-ons can make ride lines as short as 15 minutes, allowing you to ride everything on your bucket list. Also, Express Passes guests get front-section seats to Universal shows (though you have to arrive 10 to 15 minutes early to use this benefit). If you're staying at a Universal Premier Hotel, an Express Pass is included in your booking. If not, Orlando Informer sells discounted passes (*tickets.orlandoinformer.com*).

NEED TO DRY OFF?

A few Islands of Adventure water rides will leave you absolutely soaked. But near the rides' exits, you'll spot 'People Dryers.' For $6 per use, you'll get high-powered air blasted at you to dry off in record time!

– including the Forbidden Forest and Malfoy Manor – as you travel from **Hogsmeade** (MAP: 9 P102 **C1**) to the 9¾ platform in London and Diagon Alley (p95) . You might even get to enjoy some surprise Harry Potter character 'appearances' on your journey.

Don't forget to catch the Hogwarts Express both ways (p96).

Share a Meal with Your Heroes at Cafe 4

MEET & GREET

MAP: 10 P102 **E3**

Dine alongside your favorite superheroes at the **Marvel Character Dinner** (*adult/child $57/$32*). This dining experience comes with a buffet, one non-alcoholic beverage and one free photo download – and of course, the company of some of the coolest superheroes in the Marvel Universe. While the food is mediocre at best, the smiles and memories that come from this experience are worth the expense. Note that this dining experience is only offered a few times a week.

Have Breakfast with the Grinch at Circus McGurkus Cafe Stoo-pendous

MEET & GREET

MAP: 11 P102 **D1**

The holidays are your chance to eat breakfast with the grumpiest grump of them all: the Grinch – and a few of his carol-singing Who-ville friends. Officially known as **The Grinch & Friends Character Breakfast** (*adult/child, $59/33*), this meal is sometimes set up as a buffet and other times as an à la carte menu. Either way, you'll feast on Grinch-inspired dishes like Green Eggs and Ham and Cindy-Lou Who's Belgian Waffles. And don't miss the Grinch Punch. You'll want to re-serve your tickets soon after they're announced (usually mid-October to early November), because they sell out fast. Walk-ins are not available.

Take a One-Way Trip to Skull Island

THRILL RIDE

MAP: 12 P102 **B4**

Board a trackless 72-seat, open-sided vehicle 'driven' by a wise-cracking animatronic tour guide and head deep into **Skull Island**, where high-tech 3D screens bring its collection of oversized beasts to life. The biggest threat comes from a ferocious V-rex dinosaur...or is it Kong himself? Suffice it to say, it's not for the little ones.

Best Places for...

See p102 for map of locations

$ Budget $$ Midrange $$$ Top End

Eating

Sit-Down Restaurants

Mythos Restaurant $$
13 C2
Proudly displaying a banner that says 'World's Best Theme Park Restaurant,' Mythos lives up to the high expectations with its Greek-inspired bites. *11am-7pm*

Quick-Service Restaurants

Wimpy's $$
14 C3
Stop by for a Wellington Burger, a classic all-American burger with a thick, well-seasoned beef patty. *11am-6pm*

Thunder Falls Terrace $$
15 B4
Savor smoky barbecue bites like roasted pernil (slow-roasted pork) and chargrilled ribs. All combo plates also come with a refreshing chocolate, vanilla or swirled milkshake. *11am-5pm*

Green Eggs and Ham Cafe $
16 D1
All of the toppings-laden tots at this Seuss Landing eatery are worth a try, but the surprisingly delicious green-eggs-and-ham tots should be prioritized. *9am-5pm*

Natural Selections $
17 B3
Natural Selections serves up Latin American-inspired dishes. Don't miss the beef empanadas and whatever fun churro flavor is available. *hours vary*

Drinking

Harry Potter

The Butterbeer Cart
18 B1
Tucked near the crossing between Jurassic Park and the Wizarding World of Harry Potter, this little cart serves up butterbeer in both its cold and frozen variations. *11am-10pm*

Hog's Head Pub
19 B1
Inside Three Broomsticks, Hog's Head offers the best alcoholic drinks in the park. Try the Hog's Tea or one of the closely guarded secret-menu options. *8am-7pm*

Shopping

Specialty Stores

Honeydukes Candy Shop
20 B1
Magical sweets, like butterbeer fudge, butterbeer gummies, peppermint toads and love potions, await at this Hogsmeade favorite. *9am-8pm*

Owl Post
21 B1
Say hello to the Monster Book of Monsters (don't get bitten!) or send a Hogsmeade-postmarked postcard. If you're interested in the latter, bring your own stamps, as the Owl Post upcharges quite a bit. *9am-8pm*

★ WORTH A TRIP

Universal CityWalk

The gateway to the other Universal parks, **Universal CityWalk** is a pedestrian mall filled with restaurants, bars, mini-golf and shops. While you'll get a peek when entering Universal Studios (p93) and Islands of Adventure (p101), be sure to dedicate some time to explore this area.

GETTING THERE
Water taxis shuttle directly between four of the five deluxe Universal hotels and CityWalk. International Drive's I-Ride Trolley stops at nearby Universal Blvd. Paid parking is available on-site.

Scan this QR code for more information on prices, opening hours and attractions.

Food & Drink

The dining options at Universal CityWalk are so good that park-goers should exit and dine here instead. The **Cowfish Sushi Burger Bar** has long been a Universal favorite, with its unique fusion of Japanese and American cuisine. **Antojitos** is where you'll want to go for Mexican-American food. And no trip to CityWalk would be complete without a visit to the **Toothsome Chocolate Emporium & Savory Feast Kitchen** (pictured). This steampunk-inspired dessert shop has epic 2nd-floor views.

Looking for a drink? **BigFire's** whiskey-based creations are always top-notch, and **Jimmy Buffett's Margaritaville** lives up to its name. The best bar in Universal CityWalk, however, may be hidden in **Universal Great Movie Escape**. It's the only place outside of Jurassic Park (Islands of Adventure) where you can get the crowd-favorite Isla Nublar beer, along with movie-themed mocktails and cocktails.

Shopping

Despite being labeled as a shopping district, there's only one must-visit shop here: the **Universal Studios Store**. Find dinosaur plushies,

UNIVERSAL ORLANDO RESORT ©

Spiderman costumes, Harry Potter wands and other Universal merch.

Fun & Games

While CityWalk activities are often overlooked in favor of the theme parks, there are some hidden gems. **Universal Great Movie Escape** is an escape room that brings two beloved movies, *Jurassic World* and *Back to the Future*, to life. At Hollywood Drive-In Golf, choose between two 18-hole mini-golf courses for a bit of friendly competition.

For a truly exceptional experience, call CityWalk's **Hard Rock Cafe** in advance and request a tour. As the largest Hard Rock Cafe in the world, your guide will have a whole lot to share, from Jimi Hendrix's red Fender mustang guitar to a chunk of the Berlin Wall.

PARKING TIP

You pay the same pricey parking fee at CityWalk as when you're entering the theme parks. You can, however, get a reimbursement if two adults attend a matinee movie.

★ WORTH A TRIP

Volcano Bay

Transport yourself to the island of **Volcano Bay**, a tropical oasis discovered by the fictional Waturi people and home to the 200ft Krakatau Volcano. With 19 rides and attractions, this Universal Studios Resort water park is where relaxing beaches and blood-pumping thrill rides collide.

GETTING THERE
Universal Orlando hotel guests can walk or use the free shuttle bus from their hotel to the park; nonguests must get the shuttle from CityWalk (p110).

Scan this QR code for more information on prices, opening hours and attractions.

Upon Entry

When you enter, you'll be provided with complimentary TapuTapu wristbands, which eliminate most common water park issues. Use it to reserve your place in virtual queues, make in-park purchases, access your locker and more.

Kid-Friendly Fun

If you're traveling with younger kids, **Runamukka Reef** and **Tot Tiki Reef** will be your go-to areas. With geysers and water slides, spraying fountains and water cannons, your little ones will have the times of their lives. Plus, no water park day would be complete without a float down the lazy river.

If your kids are a little older, take things up a notch with **Punga Racers** or **Maku Puihi Round Raft Rides**. **Waturi Beach! Facing Krakatau** is a sandy shoreline ideal for suntanning, swimming and giving your body an adrenaline-free break.

Big Thrills

Krakatau Aqua Coaster is widely regarded as the best ride in Volcano Bay. Race through the dark corners and misty nooks of the volcano

UNIVERSAL ORLANDO RESORT ©

on a four-person canoe before crashing through a waterfall.

Volcano Bay also has a couple of drop rides, ideal for thrill-chasers. The **Ko'okiri Body Plunge** drops guests down a 125ft slide at a 70-degree angle, so it's definitely not for the faint of heart. On the slightly less intense **Kala & Tai Nui Serpentine Body Slides**, you and a partner can race to the bottom at breakneck, water-splashing speeds.

Swap drop slides for raft rides at **Honu ika Moana**. Honu is the more thrilling of the two, while ika Moana is a gentler, more family-friendly option. Last but not least, there's **TeAwa, the Fearless River**. Suit up in a life jacket and get tossed and turned on this white-water not-so-lazy river.

QUICK BREAK
Volcano Bay is known for having better-than-usual theme park fare, with an island twist. **Kohola Reef Restaurant** and **Koko Poroka Ice Cream Kona** are both great choices.

★ WORTH A TRIP

Universal Epic Universe

Brand-new in 2025, **Universal Epic Universe** is Universal Orlando Resort's newest theme park addition. It features five worlds, including the Wizarding World of Harry Potter: Ministry of Magic, How to Train Your Dragon: Isle of Berk and Super Nintendo World.

GETTING THERE
Universal Orlando Resort guests can hop on free shuttle buses to Epic Universe. Nonguests can park on-site.

Scan this QR code for more information on prices, opening hours and attractions.

An Epic Welcome

Your journey into Epic Universe begins at Chronos, the entry portal into the otherworldly Celestial Park. Serving as a through-way to the park's other worlds, this walkable area is filled with beautiful landscaping, shopping and delicious dining. But no Universal land would be complete without a few thrills, and that's where the galactic-inspired rides come into play, including the **Stardust Racers** roller coaster and the **Constellation Carousel**.

The Wizarding World of Harry Potter: Ministry of Magic

Universal Studios' big-ticket franchise is Harry Potter – it's no surprise, then, that there's another land here: the Ministry of Magic. Featuring elements of both Fantastic Beasts and the original Harry Potter series, this world seamlessly blends together 1920s France and 1990s England. You may even bump into a few magical creatures while visiting the area!

Another universe to explore is the **Isle of Berk**, which brings your *How to Train Your Dragon* dreams to life. This dragon-filled Viking village is jam-packed with attractions. Hitch a ride on a dragon on **Hiccup's Wing Gliders**, battle

UNIVERSAL ORLANDO RESORT ©

another Viking crew with water cannons on the super-soaked **Fyre Drill** and even meet Toothless himself!

Universal Favorites

In **Dark Universe**, Universal's most iconic villains have created a modern world of their own, led by none other than Dr Victoria Frankenstein, Henry Frankenstein's great-great granddaughter. Vampires, werewolves and science-experiments-gone-wrong are just the beginning of the horrors you'll stumble across in this spooky land.

Last but not least, there's **Super Nintendo World**. A fan favorite in Japan and Hollywood, this land brings your favorite Nintendo games to life, from Mario Kart to Donkey Kong.

QUICK BREAK
Rumor has it that the Universal team has put a little extra effort into the restaurants in Celestial Park, like the **Blue Dragon Pan Asian Restaurant**.

Explore Orlando & Beyond

Lake Eola Park (p135)
GABRIELE MALTINTI/GETTY ©

See p126
for eating,
drinking and
shopping
listings

Explore
Greater Orlando

It can be tempting to stick to the theme parks throughout your Orlando visit, but Greater Orlando has some real gems. Plus, the region will give both your body and wallet a break. From Winter Park and Winter Garden to Celebration and International Drive, these towns at the edges of the city are filled with all sorts of laid-back fun. Spend your days perusing local goods at farmers markets, dining at Michelin-starred restaurants and swimming in Florida's natural springs.

Getting Around

Car

For the most part, you'll need a car to get around Greater Orlando. There are some exceptions to the rule – like the adorable I-Ride Trolley on International Drive – but a car will be your primary mode of transportation.

Rideshare

If you don't want to rent a car, rideshares are widely available and, in certain cases, may be more economical.

Trolley

I-Ride Trolley services International Drive, from south of SeaWorld north to the Universal Orlando Resort area.

Blue Spring State Park (p121)

THE BEST

FARMERS MARKET Winter Park Farmers Market (p124)

MANATEE-FILLDED NATURAL SPRINGS Blue Spring State Park (p121)

ACCESSIBLE THRILL RIDE The Gator Gauntlet at Gatorland (p124)

SUSHI Norigami (p126)

U-PICK BLUEBERRY FARM Tom West Blueberries (p124)

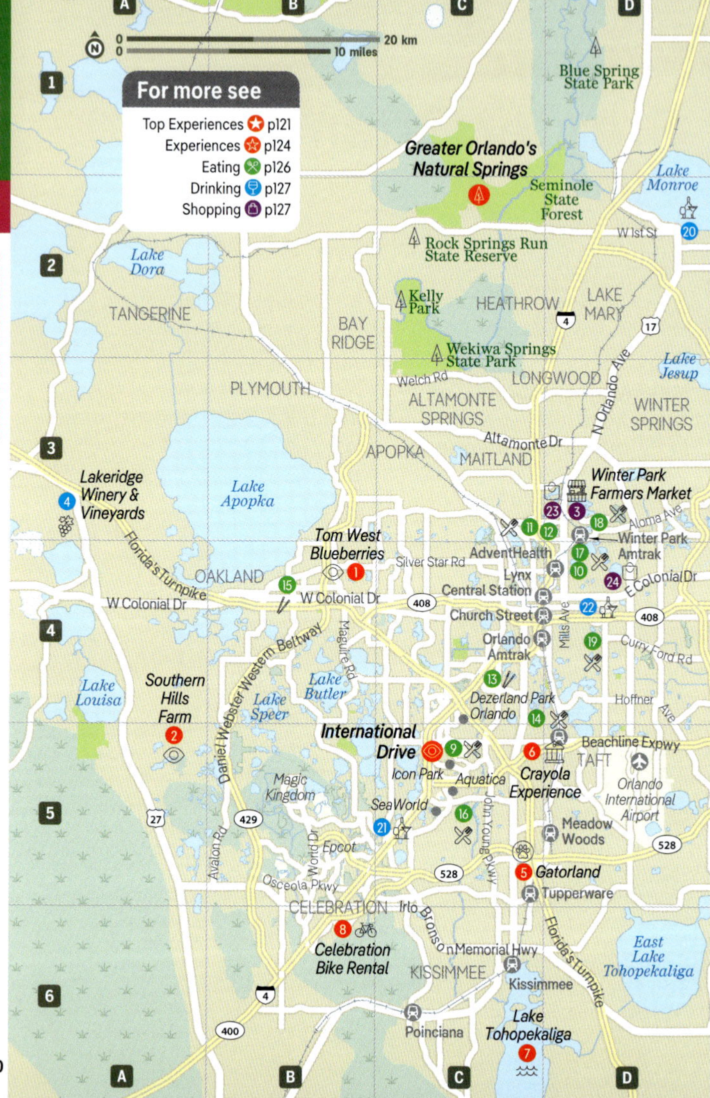
For more see
Top Experiences p121
Experiences p124
Eating p126
Drinking p127
Shopping p127
20 km
10 miles
Greater Orlando's Natural Springs
Blue Spring State Park
Seminole State Forest
Lake Monroe
W 1st St
Rock Springs Run State Reserve
Lake Dora
TANGERINE
BAY RIDGE
Kelly Park
HEATHROW
LAKE MARY
Wekiwa Springs State Park
Lake Jesup
Welch Rd
LONGWOOD
N Orlando Ave
PLYMOUTH
ALTAMONTE SPRINGS
WINTER SPRINGS
Altamonte Dr
APOPKA
MAITLAND
Lakeridge Winery & Vineyards
Lake Apopka
Winter Park Farmers Market
Aloma Ave
Winter Park Amtrak
Tom West Blueberries
Florida's Turnpike
OAKLAND
Silver Star Rd
AdventHealth
Lynx Central Station
E Colonial Dr
W Colonial Dr
W Colonial Dr
Church Street
Mills Ave
Orlando Amtrak
Curry Ford Rd
Western Beltway
Maguire Rd
Lake Louisa
Southern Hills Farm
Daniel Webster
Lake Speer
Lake Butler
Dezerland Park Orlando
Hoffner Ave
International Drive
Beachline Expwy
TAFT
Icon Park
Aquatica
Crayola Experience
Orlando International Airport
Magic Kingdom
SeaWorld
John Young Pkwy
Meadow Woods
Epcot
World Dr
Avalon Rd
Gatorland
Osceola Pkwy
Tupperware
CELEBRATION
Irlo Bronson Memorial Hwy
Celebration Bike Rental
Florida's Turnpike
East Lake Tohopekaliga
KISSIMMEE
Kissimmee
Lake Tohopekaliga
Poinciana

★ TOP EXPERIENCE

Greater Orlando's Natural Springs

Florida has thousands of stunning **natural springs**, many within driving distance of Orlando. Amid the popularity of the theme parks, they're often overlooked. But the 72°F turquoise waters and thriving greenery make for an ideal natural escape, one filled with hiking, swimming, tubing, kayaking and even manatee-spotting opportunities.

MAP **C2**

Wekiwa Springs State Park

Thirty minutes outside downtown Orlando lies **Wekiwa Springs State Park** (*floridastateparks.org; $6 per vehicle*). Whether you're hoping to hike, kayak, snorkel or swim your way through the lush greenery and emerald waters, this natural spring is ideal for a day outdoors. Wildlife thrives here; keep your eyes peeled for birds, turtles, monkeys and alligators.

Rock Springs Run State Reserve & Kelly Park

A three-for-one deal, **Rock Springs Run State Reserve** (*floridastateparks.org; $3 per vehicle*) connects the aforementioned Wekiwa Springs State Park to **Kelly Park** (*ocfl.net; $3 per vehicle*). The kayaking journey from one park to the other is magical, with stunning landscapes. The traditional trip covers 8.5 miles and takes four to five hours, though there are longer routes available.

Blue Spring State Park

Blue Spring State Park (*floridastateparks.org; $6 per vehicle*) also has incredible opportunities for swimming, kayaking, tubing and snorkeling. But what sets this spring apart are the manatees. In the colder months of the year, manatees flock to the 72°F waters of the park for warmth. On some days, you might find over 500 manatees lazing around in the turquoise waters.

PLANNING TIP

When available, check the springs' websites for updates (usually on Facebook). They'll often tell you about manatee and alligator sightings, free tours, events and more.

Scan this QR code to explore a map of Florida's 1000+ springs, both public and private.

★ TOP EXPERIENCE

International Drive

International Drive, or I-Drive for short, is Orlando's tourist hub. It's close to the theme parks, but is aimed at visitors who are taking a day off from all the roller coasters and hefty admission prices. Filled with eateries, shops and attractions, I-Drive is a great change of pace.

MAP P120 **C5**

PLANNING TIP
Use the I-Ride Trolley to get around the resort area. Making stops at just about every noteworthy attraction, this sustainable form of transport saves you the hassle and cost of parking.

Scan the QR code to purchase I-Ride trolley tickets in advance.

Ride & Dine at Icon Park

Icon Park is the heart of I-Drive, with 20 acres of family fun. The **Sea Life Orlando Aquarium** (p125) (*visitsealife.com; adult/child $25/30*) is one of the biggest draws, with 250 marine species and a 360° underwater tunnel. Then, there's the mind-bending **Museum of Illusions** (*moiorlando.com; adult/child $25/21*), where warped walls and strategically placed mirrors trick the eye. The most imposing part of Icon Park, though, is the **Orlando Eye** (*theorlandoeye.com; adult/child, $25/30*). At 400ft tall, it's Orlando's largest Ferris wheel, with views to Cape Canaveral on a clear day.

Beyond the attractions, Icon Park has a number of noteworthy dining and nightlife spots. The quick-and-casual Gordon Ramsay Fish & Chips (p126) is perfect for a midday meal. Music fans won't want to miss the Blake Shelton–owned **Ole Red**, home to concert-quality country music.

Indoor Fun at Dezerland

Florida's largest indoor attraction, **Dezerland Park Orlando** (*dezerlandpark.com; from $7 per attraction*) is jam-packed with kid-friendly activities. Bumper cars and go-karts, bowling and mini-golf, pinball machines and arcade games are just the beginning. Each activity is priced separately, so it's best to go in with a plan to avoid overspending.

THREE SIXTY IMAGES/SHUTTERSTOCK ©

The New SeaWorld Orlando

SeaWorld Orlando (*seaworld.com/orlando; from $143*) is one of the largest theme-park franchises in Orlando. When the 2013 documentary *Blackfish* was released in theaters, alleging SeaWorld's mistreatment of its captive orcas, things took a turn – both in visitor numbers and in SeaWorld's practices.

Today, SeaWorld Orlando emphasizes education and conservation, working to rehabilitate hundreds of marine animals and implementing sustainable practices across its Orlando parks. Oddly enough, SeaWorld Orlando is making a name for itself in the thrill-ride world with ocean-themed roller coasters like **Mako** and **Pipeline**. **Aquatica** (*two-day admission incl SeaWorld $215*), SeaWorld Orlando's water park, holds its own, too.

TAKE A BREAK
There's a green space right in the center of Icon Park. Order a takeout meal, snag one of the few tables and enjoy a picnic.

EXPERIENCES

Pick a Bushel of Blueberries at Tom West

FAMILY FRIENDLY

MAP: 1 P120 **B4**

Did you know that there are nearly 1000 blueberry farms in Florida? Each spring, the state bursts with blueberries, with many places offering pick-your-own experiences, including **Tom West Blueberries** (*tomwestblueberries.com*) in Ocoee. Grab a bucket or two and fill them to the brim with juicy berries. Enjoy a house-made popsicle – creamy or plain – while you're at it.

Experience Farm Fun at Southern Hills Farm

FAMILY FRIENDLY

MAP: 2 P120 **A5**

Up the ante on your farm experience with a visit to **Southern Hills Farm** (*southernhillfarms.com*) in Clermont. In addition to pick-your-own strawberries, sunflowers and veggies, there are also food stands and live music, wagon rides and a kids zone for all-day family fun.

Spend Saturday Morning at the Farmers Market

SHOP

MAP: 3 P120 **D3**

Held outside of Winter Park's historic train station, the Saturday morning **Winter Park Farmers Market** (*cityofwinterpark.org*) is always a treat. While relatively small, it's stocked to the brim with local goodies, including cheese, honey, flowers and herbs, and baked goods and fresh produce. Combine the farmers market with a stroll through downtown Winter Park's best shops, like cutesy Gasp (p127) and curated Frank (p127).

Enjoy a Free Wine Tasting at Lakeridge Winery

EAT & DRINK

MAP: 4 P120 **A3**

The **Lakeridge Winery & Vineyards** (*lakeridgewinery.com*) is the largest vineyard in Florida (127 acres). Try the fruits of their labor on a daily free tour and tasting. After a 10-minute video about the winery and the local Muscadine grapes, you can follow a guided path through the wine preservation area, sampling half a dozen wines along the way. On weekends, there's also live music and food vendors, making it the perfect spot for a picnic. It's 25 miles northwest of downtown Orlando.

Soar Over the Alligators at Gatorland

THRILL RIDE

MAP: 5 P120 **C5**

There are two zip-line experiences at **Gatorland** (*gatorland.com; adult/child $35/25*), a small-scale, alligator-based theme park. First, there's the award-winning **Screamin' Gator Zip Line**, which features five sections of zip-line totaling 1200ft of air time. There's also the **Gator Gauntlet**, which allows wheelchair users to get in on the fun. This accessible zip line zooms riders 350ft through the air – just don't look down at the 130 alligators swimming below!

Embrace Your Inner Artist at the Crayola Experience FAMILY FRIENDLY

MAP: 6 P120 C5

Have a budding artist on your hands? The **Crayola Experience** (*crayolaexperience.com; $30*) is the perfect destination for a day of creativity and fun. Unleash your inner Picasso at Modeling Madness, where you can build sculptures from colorful clay. At Scribble Square, you can literally draw on the walls without getting in trouble. Want to discover the science behind crayon-making? Catch the Crayola Factory Show (sometimes pre-recorded, sometimes live) and witness the magic of color creation. Before you leave, create a couple of epic souvenirs. Snap a family photo and have it turned into a one-of-a-kind coloring page in the Be A Star section, or name your own crayon color at Wrap It Up.

Take an Airboat Ride at Lake Tohopekaliga BOAT RIDE

MAP: 7 P120 C6

Just 45 minutes from Walt Disney World, **Lake Tohopekaliga** feels a world away. Though not part of the Everglades, this central Florida lake has many of the same natural features. Take to the swampy waters on an airboat tour and keep your eye out for all sorts of wildlife, including bald eagles, otters and, of course, alligators. Most tour operators are based either off Neptune Rd or right on the banks of the lake on Kissimmee Park Rd.

TOP PICKS FOR KIDS

Crayola Experience

see MAP: 6 P120 C5

This creative playground is filled with nearly every art-focused activity under the sun – from crayon-making to sculpture-forming to seeing the largest Crayola crayon in the world.

Southern Hills Farm

see MAP: 2 P120 A5

On top of fruit-, vegetable- and flower-picking opportunities, weekends at this Clermont farm have an array of kid-friendly activities, including carousels, tilt-a-whirls and rock-climbing walls.

Sea Life Orlando Aquarium

see MAP: 9 P120 C5

With over 250 species of marine creatures, from sharks to stingrays to seahorses, you and your little ones will leave this Icon Park attraction with a new appreciation for the underwater world.

Cycle Through Celebration NEIGHBORHOOD

MAP: 8 P120 B6

The Walt Disney Company master-planned this community in the 1990s, and Celebration continues to exude a dash of Disney magic – without the high ticket prices. Cycle your way around town, Lake Rianhard and the many hidden nature paths with the help of **Celebration Bike Rentals and Bicycle Tours**.

LISTINGS

Best Places for...

See p120 for map of locations

$ Budget $$ Midrange $$$ Top End

Eating

Quick & Casual Bites

Gordon Ramsay Fish & Chips $
9 C5
Don't miss the exceptionally airy fried fish and 'dirty' chorizo-topped fries at this grab-and-go Icon Park eatery. *11:30am-10pm Mon-Thu, 11am-11pm Fri & Sat, to 10pm Sun*

Swine & Sons $
 10 D4
Brunch, lunch and dinner with a focus on Southern comfort classics, like breakfast biscuits, fried pickles and spicy fried chicken sandwiches. *9am-8pm*

Mediterranean Deli $
 11 C3
There's no better place to get a gyro in Greater Orlando. The Greek sandwiches are affordable and flavor-packed, and it has the friendliest service in town. *10:30am-5:30pm Mon-Sat*

Hunger Street Tacos $$
12 D3
Searching for the best tacos in Greater Orlando is challenging, but this Winter Park location is certainly a contender. The brisket tacos and fried avocado tacos are tops. *11am-8pm Mon-Thu, to 9pm Fri & Sat, to 7pm Sun*

Asian Restaurants

Isan Zaap $$
13 C4
This Michelin-recognized restaurant showcases the deliciousness of northeastern Thai cuisine, with dishes like *som tum* (Thai papaya salad) and *laab* (minced pork). *11am-10pm Mon-Thu, to 10:30pm Fri & Sat*

Bombay Street Kitchen $
14 C4
This casual Indian spot is known for its great food and value. Don't miss the innovative kale chaat and street special dosa. Fantastic choice for vegan and vegetarians. *11:30am-3pm & 5-10pm*

Norigami $$$
 15 B4
Dine on exquisitely crafted sushi in Winter Garden. This eight-seat restaurant allows diners to match their favorite cuts of fish with different preparation styles. *5-9pm Tue-Thu, noon-4pm & 5-9:30pm Fri & Sat*

Authentic African

Selam Ethiopian & Eritrean Cuisine $$
16 C5
Just off I-Drive, Selam is a treat, from the lentil samosa starters to the concluding coffee ceremony. Plenty of vegan and vegetarian options, too. *noon-9pm Mon, Wed & Thu, to 10pm Fri-Sun*

Contemporary Twists

Ravenous Pig $$
17 D4
Offering innovative takes on locally sourced food American gastropub fare, this restaurant is a longtime local favorite. *4pm-late Tue-Fri, 11am-late Sat & Sun*

Prato $$$

 18 D3

Come here for modern takes on Italian classics that prioritize local and sustainable ingredients. Don't miss the meatball appetizer. *5:30-10pm Mon & Tue, 11:30am-3pm & 5:30-10pm Wed-Sun*

Papa Llama $$$

 19 D4

High-end Peruvian cuisine awaits in Orlando's Conway neighborhood. Papa Llama's multi-course tasting menu isn't cheap, but it's a Michelin-starred meal to remember. Reservations are essential. *dinner Fri & Sat*

Drinking

Cocktails

The Courtesy

 see 10 D4

Greater Orlando's first cocktail bar, the Courtesy combines speakeasy vibes with thoughtfully crafted drinks. *4pm-midnight Tue-Thu, to 1am Fri & Sat, 3-10pm Sun, 6pm-midnight Mon*

Suffering Bastard

 20 D2

Savor cutting-edge tropical cocktails at this controversially named tiki bar bar. And if you really love your cocktail glass or mug, they're for sale. *5-10pm Wed, Thu & Sun, to midnight Fri & Sat*

More Than Drinks

Player 1 Video Game Bar

 21 C5

This Lake Buena Vista arcade bar is filled with nearly every video game in existence – from retro arcade style to modern PlayStation, Wii and Xbox. Don't miss the Asian-inspired cocktails. *1pm-2am*

Otto's High Dive

 22 D4

Located in the Milk District, Otto's High Dive is a restaurant known more for its drinks than its impressive cuisine. It specializes in rum: the guava pastelito and coquito cocktails are absolutely incredible. *4pm-midnight Tue-Sat, 11am-10pm Sun*

Shopping

Specialty Stores

Bossa N' Roll Records

23 D3

Leaning into Orlando's old-school purchase preferences, Bossa N' Roll in Maitland has a well-curated selection of vinyl. *11am-7pm Tue-Sat*

Atomic Horror

24 D4

A haven for horror enthusiasts, this niche shop has all sorts of spooky memorabilia and merchandise from beloved horror film franchises. *11am-7pm*

Lifestyle Boutiques

Frank

 see 18 D3

Charming gift shop in downtown Winter Park, showcasing curated goods like precious stone-based jewelry and beachy coconut wax candles. *10am-6pm Mon-Sat, noon-5pm Sun*

Gasp

 see 18 D3

Girly pop core at its finest, this boutique is filled with stationery, accessories, home decor and more, all created by small-scale artists. *10am-6pm Sun-Thu, to 8 pm Fri & Sat*

See p137
for eating, drinking and shopping listings

Explore
Downtown Orlando

Most visitors to Orlando rarely venture beyond the fabricated worlds of Walt Disney World® and Universal Orlando, yet the city of Orlando is home to gardens, nature preserves, fabulous cuisine, great cocktail bars and a delightfully slower pace. Downtown Orlando also has a vibrant arts scene, with numerous galleries and theaters, as well as lively festivals and events throughout the year. Take time to admire the historic architecture, and seek hidden treasures as you browse the local boutiques and markets. Whether you're a foodie, an art lover or simply looking to unwind, downtown Orlando has something for everyone.

Getting Around

Bus

LYMMO is the downtown Orlando circulator bus, providing free public transportation in the downtown business, entertainment and shopping district.

Bike Share

With hundreds of dockless bikes across Orlando, HOPR Bike Share is the best way to get around while having fun in Orlando. Download the HOPR Transit app, scan the QR code on the bike or scooter, and cycle around town to your heart's content. To end your ride, lock the wheel and let the app know you've reached your destination.

THE BEST

ENTERTAINMENT Orlando Shakespeare Theater (p134)

SHOPPING Orlando Farmers Market (p134)

CULTURAL EXPERIENCE Wells' Built Museum (p134)

OUTDOOR FUN Lake Eola Park (p135)

DINING Little Saigon (p136)

Lake Eola
SONGQUAN DENG/SHUTTERSTOCK ©

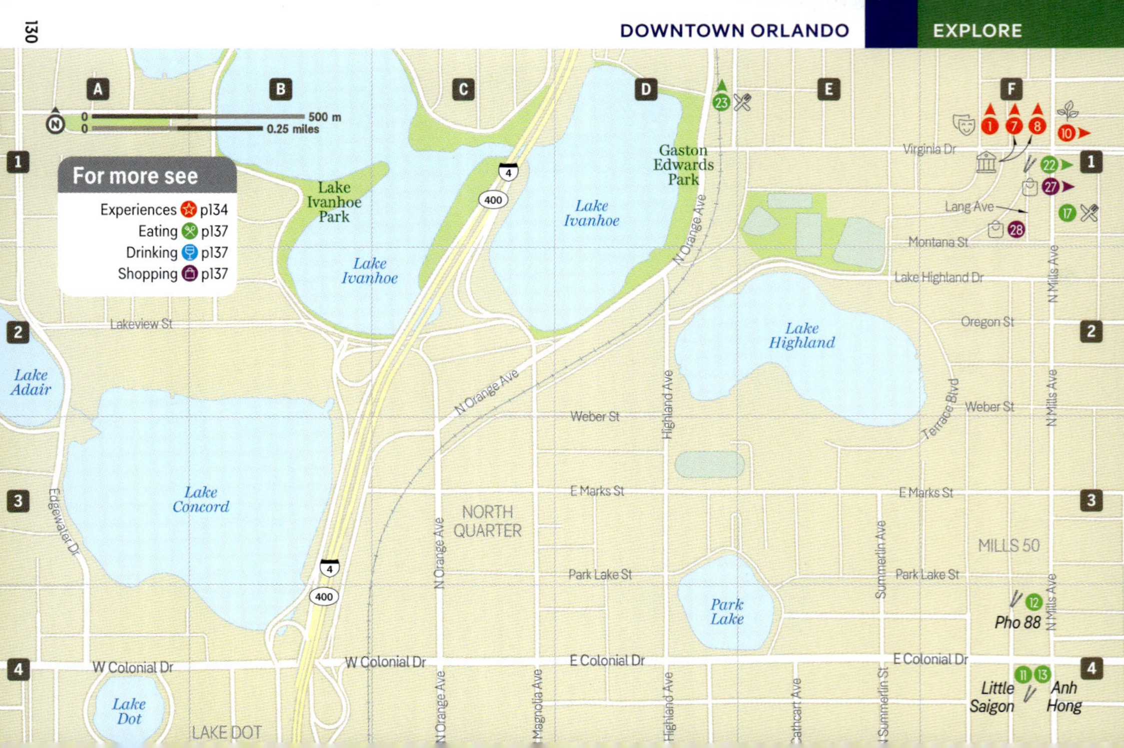
For more see
Experiences p134
Eating p137
Drinking p137
Shopping p137
500 m
0.25 miles
Lake Ivanhoe Park
Lake Ivanhoe
Gaston Edwards Park
Lake Highland
Lake Adair
Lake Concord
Park Lake
Lake Dot
NORTH QUARTER
MILLS 50
LAKE DOT
Lakeview St
Virginia Dr
Lang Ave
Montana St
Lake Highland Dr
Oregon St
Weber St
Terrace Blvd
E Marks St
Park Lake St
N Orange Ave
Highland Ave
N Mills Ave
Summerlin Ave
Edgewater Dr
W Colonial Dr
E Colonial Dr
Magnolia Ave
Cathcart Ave
Pho 88
Little Saigon
Anh Hong

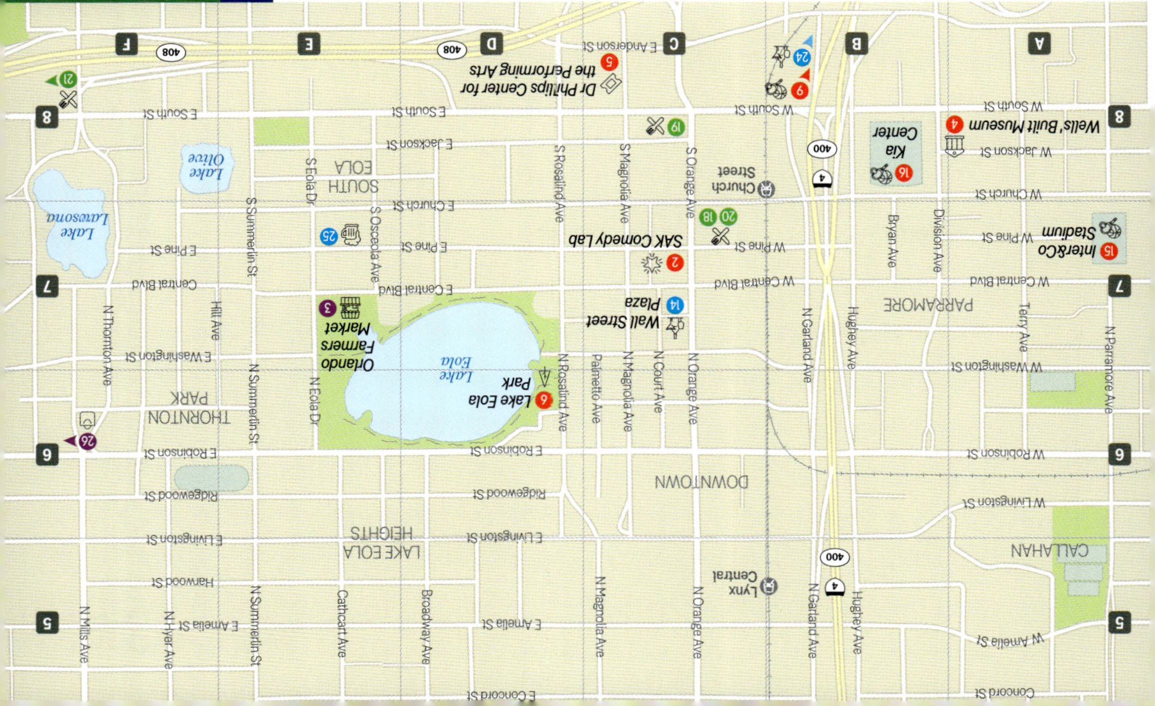

Dr Phillips Center for the Performing Arts 5
Wells' Built Museum 4
Kia Center 16
Church Street
SAK Comedy Lab 2
Inter&Co Stadium 15
Wall Street Plaza 14
Orlando Farmers Market 3
Lake Eola Park 6
Lake Eola
Lake Lawsona
Lake Olive
Lynx Central
SOUTH EOLA
THORNTON PARK
PARRAMORE
DOWNTOWN
LAKE EOLA HEIGHTS
CALLAHAN
9
19
18
20
21
24
25
26
E Anderson St
E South St
W South St
E Jackson St
W Jackson St
E Church St
W Church St
E Pine St
W Pine St
Central Blvd
E Central Blvd
W Central Blvd
E Washington St
W Washington St
E Robinson St
W Robinson St
Ridgewood St
E Livingston St
W Livingston St
Harwood St
E Amelia St
W Amelia St
E Concord St
Concord St
N Thornton Ave
Hill Ave
S Summerlin St
N Summerlin St
S Eola Dr
N Eola Dr
S Osceola Ave
S Rosalind Ave
N Rosalind Ave
Palmetto Ave
S Magnolia Ave
N Magnolia Ave
N Court Ave
S Orange Ave
N Orange Ave
N Garland Ave
Hughey Ave
Bryan Ave
Division Ave
Terry Ave
N Parramore Ave
N Mills Ave
N Hyer Ave
Cathcart Ave
Broadway Ave
408
400
4
A
B
C
D
E
F
5
6
7
8

WALKING TOUR

A Night Out in Downtown Orlando

Downtown Orlando truly comes alive at night, with music pouring out of the bars and sidewalk tables filled up with lingerers. The college-town energy grows as the night progresses. This local crawl will guide you to some of the most laid-back spots beyond the usual happy-hour frenzy.

START	END	LENGTH
The Woods	Mad Cow Theatre	1 mile; 6 hours

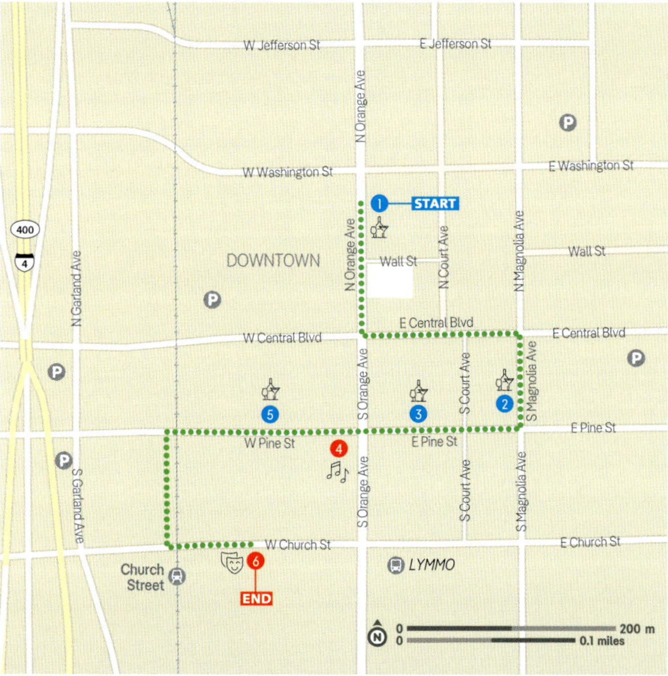

1 Cocktails in the Woods

Get into the night's spirit with a Vanishing Glass or a Dingle Hopper at **The Woods**, on the 2nd floor of the Historic Rose Building, which has exposed brick, a tree-trunk bar and an earthy feel. The Woods is known for its unusual libations made from small-batch distilleries and house-made syrups and infusions.

2 Speakeasy Sophistication

Elevate your cocktail experience with a drink made just as it would have been in the 1920s at **Mathers Social Gathering**, a beautifully designed bar on the 3rd floor of a 19th-century building. This is one of the most beautiful bars in town.

3 Additional Speakeasy Secrets

For another hidden gem, visit **Hanson's Shoe Repair**, which requires a password for entry. This intimate spot embraces the Prohibition-era speakeasy theme, down to the historically accurate cocktails. Once inside, it's a cozy nest of folks having a quiet good time.

4 Live Music

Take it up a notch at **Tanqueray's Bar & Grille**, an unpretentious underground haunt that was formerly a bank vault. It can get smoky and loud, but this little dive plays some of the best live local music in town.

5 Halloween Mayhem

It's Halloween every night at **Cocktails & Screams**, which welcomes freaks and Gothic geeks with a regular schedule of themed events. On Wednesdays, you'll find yourself among Addams Family look-alikes. Look for clues on the walls to find the secret 'coven bar' entrance.

6 Take in a Play

If you need a break from the nightlife, catch a performance at the venerable **Mad Cow Theatre**. This intimate regional playhouse regularly earns rave reviews for its stagings of local playwrights, theater classics such as *Cat on a Hot Tin Roof* and Broadway hits.

EXPERIENCES

Catch a Play at the Orlando Shakespeare Theater
SHOW

MAP: 1 P130 **F1**

The **Orlando Shakespeare Theater** showcases the Bard's legacy by bringing fan-favorite musicals, compelling dramas and engaging children's plays to the stage, including the original Elizabethan production of *Twelfth Night* performed in 17th-century English. The **John & Rita Lowndes Shakespeare Center** (*orlandoshakes.org*) houses Orlando Shakes and four theater spaces (the Margeson, Goldman, Mandell and Santos-Dantin Studio theaters).

Laugh the Night Away at SAK Comedy Lab
SHOW

MAP: 2 P131 **C7**

The hilarious ensemble of improv actors at **SAK Comedy Lab** (*sakcomedylab.com*) hits the stage of this 250-seat theater almost every night. They take audience suggestions and invent characters, scenes and songs on the spot. Fun and edgy for adults and mature teens, some of the gags might fly over the heads of younger fans.

Shop for Tropical Bounty at the Farmers Market
EAT & DRINK

MAP: 3 P131 **E7**

Every Sunday from 10 am to 3 pm visitors flock to Lake Eola Park for the lakeside **Orlando Farmers Market** (*orlandofarmersmarket.com*). Some 50 vendors sell local produce and gourmet cheeses, handmade soaps and jewelry, flower bouquets and freshly squeezed juices, all to the beat of live music. Bring a blanket and plan to picnic with your goodies under the shade of a tree or on one of the many benches in Lake Eola Park.

Learn about Orlando's African American History at the Wells' Built Museum
CULTURAL

MAP: 4 P131 **A8**

Located in the center of Orlando's historic Parramore district, the small **Wells' Built Museum** (*wellsbuilt.org; adult/child $5/3*) is dedicated to Orlando's African American history and culture. It's housed in the former Wells' Hotel, built in 1921 by Dr William Monroe Wells to host African American performers forbidden from staying in the city's strictly segregated accommodations. Through its doors passed many an influential performer, including Count Basie, Cab Calloway, Billie Holiday, Ella Fitzgerald and Duke Ellington. On the top floor you'll find a hotel room frozen in time, complete with the furniture and decor that would have greeted guests in the 1930s.

See a Musical at the Dr Phillips Center for the Performing Arts
SHOW

MAP: 5 P131 **C8**

The **Dr Phillips Center for the Performing Arts** (*drphillips* *center.org*) is downtown Orlando's premier venue for live entertainment. It features three state-of-the-art theaters and an outdoor plaza, hosting a range of performances from Broadway shows to ballet, comedy and concerts. A nonprofit organization, it champions Arts For Every Life, offering educational programs and community events.

Paddle a Swan Boat at Lake Eola Park

PARK

MAP: 6 P131 **D6**

Pretty and shaded, flower-filled **Lake Eola Park** sits between downtown Orlando and Thorton Park. A paved sidewalk 0.9 miles in length circles the lake, there's a waterfront playground and you can rent swan paddleboats to meet the many real swans that live here. On the west side of the lake, the **Walt Disney Amphitheater** hosts concerts, movies and plays.

Enjoy Hands-On Fun at Orlando Science Center

CULTURAL

MAP: 7 P130 **F1**

The **Orlando Science Center** (*osc.org; adult/child $24/18*) is a hands-on science museum. Four floors of interactive exhibit halls invite children (ages 5 to 12) and adults to step into the prehistoric world of dinosaurs, explore the complexities of our food system and test the fundamentals of electricity and gravity. Don't miss the observatory, which houses Florida's largest public refractor telescope.

Check Out the Orlando Museum of Art

CULTURAL

MAP: 8 P130 **F1**

Founded in 1924 by local art enthusiasts, the **Orlando Museum of Art** (*OMA; omart.org; adult/child $20/8*) showcases over 2400 objects, including contemporary art, American art from the 18th century to 1945, African art and the art of the ancient Americas. The museum also hosts adult and family-friendly art events and classes.

Catch a Game at the ESPN Wide World of Sports

SPORTS

MAP: 9 P131 **B8**

Disney delved deep into the wide world of sports when it opened its $100 million, 220-acre multi-sports complex in 1997. Welcoming amateur and pro athletes from around the world, the nine venues at the **ESPN Wide World of Sports** (*espnwwos.com*) host more than 100 annual athletic events, with more than 70 different sports for amateur and professional athletes.

Visit the Harry P Leu Gardens

GARDEN

MAP: 10 P130 **F1**

Stroll the 50-acre **Leu Gardens** (*leugardens.org; adult/child $15/10*), an impressive botanical oasis just minutes from downtown Orlando. The plant collection includes cycads (primitive plants that have existed for nearly 200 million years), bright red hibiscus and almost 400 species of palm trees. The citrus grove's 50 different kinds of citrus trees highlight Florida's agricultural bounty, while the native wetland garden hosts wading birds and other wildlife. Tours of the 18th-century **Leu House** run every half hour. Bring provisions for a lakeside picnic.

Explore Little Saigon

CULTURAL

In the 1970s, many Vietnamese settled north of downtown Orlando, revitalizing the area with small businesses. Today, a 10-block stretch of Colonial Drive near Mills Avenue is lined with Vietnamese restaurants, shops and markets. The area also features Chinese, Thai, Korean and other Asian establishments, along with medical and dental offices, nail salons, travel agencies, health food centers, martial arts studios, boba tea shops, music and video stores, a karaoke bar and a martial arts weapons store.

This neighborhood, once known as Little Saigon, is now called the Mills 50 District as part of the Orlando Main Street Program. The new name reflects the intersection of Mills Ave and Colonial Dr but doesn't fully capture the area's unique character. Three restaurants worth checking out include **Little Saigon** (MAP: 11 P130 **F4**) (best for pho, rice noodle soup), **Pho 88** (MAP: 12 P130 **F4**) (also good for pho, as well as bun bo hue, a spicy beef noodle soup) and **Anh Hong** (MAP: 13 P130 **F4**) (famous for its bánh bèo, savory steamed rice cakes).

Party at Wall Street Plaza

NIGHTLIFE

MAP: 14 P131 **C7**

Party all night long at **Wall Street Plaza** (*wallstplaza.net*), a vibrant entertainment hub featuring a variety of bars, restaurants and nightclubs. You can enjoy a night out dancing, drinking and socializing in venues like **Hooch**, a tiki bar; **Sideshow**, a carnival-themed bar where you play games to determine your drink; and **The Attic**, a dance club in an old moonshine warehouse.

Cheer on the Orlando Pride

SPORTS

MAP: 15 P131 **A7**

The Orlando City Soccer Club, founded in 2013, is a Major League Soccer (MLS) team known for its passionate fan base. The club also includes the Orlando Pride, a professional women's soccer team in the National Women's Soccer League (NWSL), and Orlando City B, a youth development team. Catch a game at **Inter&Co Stadium** (*interco-stadium.com*), a 25,500-seat soccer-specific stadium.

Go Courtside with the Orlando Magic

SPORTS

MAP: 16 P131 **B8**

Kia Center (*kiacenter.com*) is a premier indoor arena hosting a variety of events. Home to the NBA's Orlando Magic, the ECHL's Orlando Solar Bears and the National Arena League's Orlando Predators, it also hosts concerts, family shows, and other entertainment events.

LISTINGS

Best Places for...

See p130 for map of locations

$ Budget $$ Midrange $$$ Top End

Eating

Restaurants

Black Rooster Taqueria $$
17 F1
A counter-service favorite that serves up tasty Mexican fare at a quick pace. BYOB. *11am-2pm & 5-10pm Tue-Sun*

Kres Chophouse $$$
18 C7
Kres Chophouse is a modern steakhouse is known for its eclectic steak and seafood dishes. *11:30am-11pm Mon-Fri, from 5pm Sat & Sun*

The Boheme $$$
19 C8
Situated in the elegant Grand Bohemian Hotel, the Boheme serves sophisticated American fare in an art-centric ambience. *7am-2pm & 5-10pm*

Artisan's Table $$
 C7
Chow down on a breakfast bowl of eggs and grits, or steel-cut oats with agave and an organic smoothie. *11am-9pm*

Pizza Bruno $$
 F8
Bruno dishes out some of the best pizzas in town, with a focus on seasonal ingredients. *noon-9:30pm*

Domu $$
 F1
Popular ramen spot that makes its own noodles. *5-10pm Mon-Fri, 11am-2:30pm & 5-10pm Sat & Sun*

White Wolf Cafe & Bar $$
 D1
This gourmet bistro features Tiffany-style chandeliers, a long wooden bar and a mishmash of antiques. *8am-2:30pm Sun-Wed, to 9pm Thu-Sat*

Drinking

Bars

Icebar
 B8
Sit on an ice seat and sip icy drinks at the Icebar. *5pm-midnight Sun-Thu, to 2am Fri & Sat*

Stubborn Mule
 E7
Popular gastropub that serves handcrafted cocktails and contemporary cuisine. Live music on weekends. *11am-10pm*

Shopping

Souvenirs

Etoile Boutique
26 F6
Sells vintage clothing and handmade jewelry, making it a hub for fashion and pop culture enthusiasts. *6-10pm Tue, noon-7pm Wed-Sat*

Primrose Shop
27 F1
Specializes in personalized gifts and is known for its charming selection of accessories. *10am-5:30pm Mon-Sat*

House on Lang
 F1
Stop by for a creative workshop or to browse fashion, local art, gifts and home decor. *10am-7pm Mon-Sat, noon-6pm Sun*

★ WORTH A TRIP

Kennedy Space Center

One of Florida's most visited attractions, the **Kennedy Space Center** (*kennedyspacecenter.com; adult/child $75/65*) was once the country's primary space-flight facility, where shuttles were built and astronauts rocketed into the cosmos. Although NASA terminated its shuttle program in 2011, regular rocket launches still take place here.

GETTING THERE
The Kennedy Space Center is 50 miles east of Orlando on Merritt Island; parking is $15 for the day. To get around the complex, use the complimentary shuttles or walking paths.

Scan this QR code for more information on prices, opening hours and attractions.

Visitor Complex

The **Visitor Complex**, with several exhibits showcasing the history and future of US space travel and research, is the heart of the Kennedy Space Center. Here you'll find the **Rocket Garden**, featuring replicas of classic rockets towering over the complex; **Heroes & Legends** and the US Astronaut Hall of Fame, with films and multimedia exhibits honoring astronauts; and the hour-long **Astronaut Encounter**, where a real, live astronaut fields questions from the audience. A NASA Now exhibit includes **Journey to Mars**, a collection of shows and interactive exhibits dedicated to the latest plans for exploring the Red Planet, including Mars rover replicas, and **Gateway: the Deep Space Launch Complex**, which explores the latest innovations in deep space travel. Two delightful IMAX films are included in admission.

The stunningly beautiful **Space Mirror Memorial**, a shiny granite wall standing four stories high, reflects both literally and figuratively on the personal and tragic stories behind the Kennedy Space Center.

NADEZDA MURMAKOVA/SHUTTERSTOCK ©

Kennedy Space Center Bus Tour

The bus tour to the **Apollo/Saturn V Center** (pictured) consists of a 20-minute ride through restricted areas, showcasing iconic sites like the Vehicle Assembly Building and Launching Pad Complex. The tour is narrated by experts and includes views of historic launch sites. Upon arrival, visitors can explore the Apollo/Saturn V Center, which houses a massive Saturn V rocket, interactive exhibits and the Moon Rock Cafe. Tours depart every 15 minutes; count on two hours total.

ADD-ON TOURS

For an additional cost, you can visit the Vehicle Assembly Building, Cape Canaveral Air Force Station and its launch sites and the Launch Control Center, where engineers perform system checks.

Space Shuttle Atlantis

Blasted by rocket fuel and streaked with space dust, **space shuttle Atlantis**, the final orbiter among NASA's fleet, is the most impressive exhibit in the complex. Suspended in a specially

TAKE A BREAK
Situated at the Apollo/Saturn V Center, the **Moon Rock Cafe** has indoor and outdoor seating with views of historic spacecraft.

designed $100-million space, it hangs just a few feet out of reach, its nose down and payload doors open, as if it's still orbiting the Earth. It's a creative and dramatic display, preceded by a chest-swelling film that tells the story of the shuttle program from its inception in the 1960s to *Atlantis'* final mission in 2011. Around the shuttle, interactive consoles invite visitors to try to land it or dock it at the International Space Station, touchscreens offer details of missions and crews, and there's a full-size replica of the Hubble Space Telescope and a not-very-scary 'shuttle launch experience.' Docents, many of whom worked on the shuttle program, are stationed around the exhibits to answer questions and tell tall space tales.

NADEZDA MURMAKOVA/SHUTTERSTOCK ©

See a Real Rocket Launch

Watching a **rocket launch** is an unforgettable experience. You can choose from several viewing locations, such as the LC-39 Observation Gantry, Banana Creek Launch Viewing Area or the Apollo/Saturn V Center lawn. Each location offers a unique perspective and live commentary from space experts.

To secure a spot, you can purchase Launch Transportation Tickets (LTTs) or special launch viewing packages, which include admission and additional perks. Book these in advance as they sell out quickly.

For the latest schedule of upcoming launches, visit the Kennedy Space Center's official launch schedule on its website.

Meet an Astronaut

The **Astronaut Encounter** offers a rare opportunity to meet veteran NASA astronauts. During this 40-minute experience, astronauts share their space missions and answer audience questions in a live presentation. Held in the Universe Theater, the session includes a photo opportunity and autograph session with the astronaut of the day. For a more intimate experience, the 'Chat with an Astronaut' program allows small groups to engage in casual conversations over snacks.

Souvenirs

The **Space Shop** is the world's largest store dedicated to space memorabilia and NASA gear, including astronaut suits, space-themed apparel and mission patches. You can also find rare collectibles like genuine meteorites and models of historic rockets. The 2nd floor features the original Apollo 11 gantry, where you can walk in the footsteps of astronauts.

SPACE ICE CREAM

For that quintessential astronaut experience, don't miss space ice cream. A freeze-dried treat that was developed for astronauts to enjoy in space, it has no water content, making it lightweight and shelf-stable without refrigeration. Try some at the **Milky Way** ice-cream shop, which sells a variety of styles, including traditional scoops and fun creations like the Rings of Saturn.

Legoland®

Legoland® is a joy. With manageable crowds and lines, this lakeside theme park maintains an old-school vibe – you don't have to plan like a general to enjoy a day here, and it's strikingly stress-free and relaxed. It's best for kids aged 2 to 12.

GETTING THERE
Legoland® is 50 miles southwest of Orlando, in Winter Haven. It's roughly 1¼ hours by car from the city. The Legoland Shuttle (*$10*) runs daily from I-Drive 360.

Scan this QR code for more information on prices, opening hours and attractions.

Rides & Shows

Highlights at Legoland® (*legoland.com; admission from $74*) include **Flight School**, a coaster that zips you around with your feet dangling free, **Miniland**, a Lego recreation of iconic American landmarks and cities, and **Ninjago**, the park's martial-arts-themed section. Little thrill-seekers will want to give the VR-enhanced **Great Lego Race** a go. There are a few remnants from the park's history as the site of Cypress Gardens (c 1936), including lovely botanical gardens with the giant Banyan tree, water-ski shows and a classic wooden roller coaster, these days called **Coastersaurus**. The water-ski show centers on a bizarre and silly pirate theme.

Don't miss the **Imagination Zone**, a wonderful interactive learning center that's staffed with skilled Lego makers happy to help children of all ages create delights with their blocks.

The Big Shop

Don't leave Legoland® without stopping by the **Big Shop**. Located in the entrance area, it offers the ultimate Lego shopping experience, including a fine selection of rare and exclusive Lego sets that you

DOUBLE2A/SHUTTERSTOCK ©

won't find anywhere else. Create your own custom minifigure with unique accessories and outfits.

Join Peppa Pig

Toddlers and preschoolers won't want to miss the world's first **Peppa Pig Theme Park** (*peppapigthemepark.com; admission $39*), situated steps away from Legoland. Themed playscapes, water play areas, character meet-and-greets and tame rides will delight young kids. Take a ride on **Daddy Pig's Roller Coaster**, a perfect first roller coaster or set sail in search of hidden treasure aboard the kid-sized boats on **Grandad Dog's Pirate Boat Ride**. It's possible to purchase Legoland® combo tickets.

QUICK BREAK

No amusement-park trip is complete without a funnel cake. Try one at the **Funnel Cake Factory**, where the cakes are topped with powdered sugar, strawberries or chocolate.

Orlando & Walt Disney World® Resort Toolkit

Eola Lake (p135)

Family Travel

Orlando is the epitome of a kid-friendly destination. From theme parks to hotels to restaurants, the city's most popular sites are sure to keep little ones entertained.

Discounted Tickets

Both Walt Disney World® and Universal Orlando offer slightly discounted prices for children between the ages of three and nine (children under three get in free). General admission to Legoland Orlando and SeaWorld Orlando is the same for both kids and adults.

REST DAYS

While you may be tempted to hit the big parks every day, don't forget to give your kids (and your wallet) a break. Visit some of Central Florida's **natural springs**, walk through **Universal CityWalk** or **Disney Springs**, or just spend a day by the hotel pool instead.

Strollers: To Rent or Not to Rent?

If you have young kids, you'll need a stroller to navigate the big parks. The question is, should you rent one at the parks, bring your own or rent one from an outside provider, like Kingdom Strollers or Scooterbug? For the best balance of price and convenience, most families opt for the latter option.

Child Swap

If a child isn't tall enough to ride, the child swap program allows one parent to stay with them while others go on the ride. The parent can then go on the ride without having to queue.

Kids Menus

The vast majority of restaurants in Orlando have dedicated kids menus, and even the pickiest of eaters will find meals to enjoy.

Height Restrictions

All Orlando theme parks have height restrictions for at least some of the rides. You'll often find these marked at the start of the ride line, or you can check the respective website or app.

Accommodations

Orlando welcomes 74 million visitors annually, meaning that there are lots of accommodation choices for all budgets.

Where to Stay if You Love...

Disney Perks

Walt Disney World® Resort (p32) Home to dozens of impeccably themed hotels. Depending on the hotel, you may get perks like early park access, extended hours and priority dining.

Universal Studios Benefits

Universal Orlando Resort (p88) Several well-located hotels have free transportation across Universal. Depending on the hotel, you may get early park access, pool-hopping perks and express passes.

Dining & Nightlife

Downtown Orlando (p129) and **Mills 50** (p136) These two neighborhoods are Orlando's nightlife and dining hot spots and are great options for foodies and night owls.

Budget Choices & Family Fun

I-Drive (p122) If you're only spending part of your trip at the theme parks, stay on I-Drive, where many restaurants, shops and other attractions are located.

Quiet Nights & a Dash of Pixie Dust

Celebration (p125) Developed by the Walt Disney Company in the 1990s, this neighborhood is the perfect blend of quiet evenings and Disney magic.

We Love to Stay in...

Lake Buena Vista. Located just a short drive away from the most popular Orlando attractions – Walt Disney World® (p32), Universal Orlando Resort (p88) and I-Drive (p122) – Lake Buena Vista provides easy access to the city's best options. And yet it's still relatively peaceful, perfect for a poolside rest day.

HOW MUCH FOR A NIGHT IN

Hostel **$30**

Typical midrange hotel **$180**

Midrange theme park hotel **$300**

Food, Drink & Nightlife

Allergies & Intolerances

Many sit-down restaurants in Orlando will ask about allergies when you order. Be sure to make dietary restrictions clear in advance. Theme parks have allergen information lists at their restaurants, and Walt Disney World® has special diet-trained cast members. Each major theme park also has a dedicated email for those with dietary restrictions who need assistance: special.diets@disneyworld.com, allergenfriendlyswf@seaworld.com and foodservicecuf@universalorlando.com.

ALLIGATOR FOR DINNER?

You'll likely spot this reptile on a number of Orlando restaurant menus, usually in the form of nugget-like 'gator bites.' Surprisingly, it's delicious when prepared properly.

THEME PARK DINING PLANS

Walt Disney World® Resort, Universal Orlando Resort and SeaWorld Orlando all offer some version of a dining plan. When used on pricier items or for large groups, these plans can help you save a pretty penny.

Theme Park Reservations

The most popular theme park restaurants, like **Be Our Guest** in Disney's Magic Kingdom and **Mythos** in Universal's Islands of Adventure, often get booked up weeks or months in advance. The same applies to the restaurants in **Disney Springs** (p79) and **Universal CityWalk** (p110). Make reservations early using the parks' websites and apps.

HOW TO... Pay the Bill

Asking for the bill Waitstaff will usually provide the bill unprompted. If not, a quick hand-raise and 'Can I get the check, please?' will do the trick.

Splitting the bill Assuming you don't have an overly large party, most restaurants in Orlando will be happy to split the bill.

Paying the bill While many restaurants stick with the tried-and-true paper receipt method, several have gone digital, whether through remote scanners or QR codes.

Tipping When dining at sit-down restaurants, the standard tip ranges from 15% to 20%, though norms are shifting to the higher end.

PRICE RANGES

The following price ranges refer to the average cost of a main course, before the tip.

$ less than $17

$$ $17–32

$$$ more than $32

OPENING HOURS

Cafes 7am to 6pm

Restaurants 11am to 10pm

Bars 4pm to midnight Monday to Friday, noon to 2am Saturday and Sunday

Going Out

Theme park shopping districts

While most theme parks close a few hours after sunset, their shopping districts, like Universal CityWalk, Disney Springs and Disney Boardwalk, stay open much later. Find everything from dueling pianos to classic cocktails to lively clubs here.

Out-of-the-box bars

While you can certainly find a classy lounge or casual sports bar, Orlando has more than its fair share of unique nightspots as well. Player 1 Orlando is an arcade bar filled with nearly every video game in existence. On I-Drive, Icebar Orlando – part-bar, part-nightclub – cools things down in its below-freezing venue, while also heating things up in the Fire Lounge.

Rules & regulations

In recent years, the city of Orlando has passed many laws that aren't conducive to nightlife. For example, parking garages close at 11pm on weekends and establishments now need special permits to serve alcohol after midnight.

HOW MUCH FOR A

Coffee From $3

Quick-service theme-park meal $15–20

Street taco From $2 each

Grouper sandwich $20–25

Sit-down theme-park entree From $20

Glass of butterbeer $10

Glass of wine $10–15

Scoop of ice cream $4–7

LGBTIQ+ Travelers

Orlando was once one of the more LGBTIQ+-friendly destinations in the USA, though recent Florida state legislation has led to an erosion of rights, particularly for transgender people.

Pride Events

Girls in Wonderland (May & June) A lively music festival and pool party, dedicated to the coolest lesbian and queer artists around.

One Magical Weekend (May & June) A multiday music festival for the LGBTIQ+ community, held at Walt Disney World®.

GayDays Orlando (June) A massive five-day celebration. Theme park days and parties often take place at Walt Disney World®, Universal Orlando and SeaWorld Orlando.

Red Shirt Pride Day (June) Taking place since 1991, on the first Saturday in June, participants wear red and meet in front of Cinderella's Castle in Magic Kingdom for a day of theme-park fun with like-minded friends.

Come Out with Pride (October) The city's official pride celebration, filled with parades, firework shows and more.

PULSE MEMORIAL

On June 12, 2016, 49 people were killed and 53 wounded at a mass shooting at Orlando's LGBTIQ+ Pulse nightclub. A temporary memorial stands at the downtown Orlando Health location.

OUR PICKS

LGBTIQ+ Cafes, Bars & Clubs

Easy Luck Coffee & Bodega / Whippoorwill Beer House Trendy coffee shop by day, curated beer house by night, LGBTIQ+-friendly all the time.

Savoy Orlando A longtime LGBTIQ+ bar and nightclub with dancers and drag shows.

Southern Nights Often called Orlando's best gay bar and club.

THE RENAISSANCE THEATER COMPANY

Known for its innovative (and often adult) plays, productions, and performances, the 'Ren' is a hot spot for the LGBTIQ+ community.

Resources

• **visitorlando.com/plan/culture-diversity/lgbtq** LGBTIQ+ travel page from the official Visit Orlando tourism board. • **villatel.com/journal/exploring-gay-orlando** Well-written LGBTIQ+ travel page an Orlando vacation rental company. • **thecenter orlando.org** An LGBTIQ+ support and advocacy group.

Health & Safe Travel

Orlando is a relatively safe place to travel, but you should be aware of weather conditions, wildlife and common scams.

THUNDERSTORMS

Thunderstorms are a common weather phenomenon in Orlando, particularly during summer afternoons. Pools and many theme park rides will close for safety whenever thunder and lightning are present. It's best to head inside and wait until the storm passes.

Hurricanes

While Orlando is an inland city, hurricanes can still have an impact, especially during the storm season from June through November. Direct hits are uncommon, but indirect effects like strong winds and heavy rain are likely. If you're visiting during hurricane season, stay informed. Check reliable sources like the **National Hurricane Center** (*nhc.noaa.gov*) and **National Weather Service** (*weather.gov*) for updates. Follow all official instructions.

Heat

From June to September, temperatures are regularly in the 90s, with humidity around 75%.

Wildlife

From alligators to snakes to panthers, there's a whole lot of wildlife in Florida. It's unlikely that you'll encounter any of these in the theme parks, but you may cross paths with an animal at a nearby natural spring. The rule of thumb is: if you leave them alone, they'll leave you alone.

THEME PARK SCAMS

There are two common ticket scams: counterfeit tickets and 'sales' on the remaining days of a multiday pass. Always buy your tickets directly from the theme parks.

SECURITY MEASURES

Metal detectors

All guests must pass through metal detectors before entering a theme park.

Bag checks

Most bags will undergo a quick, manual screening by security.

Lockers

On the most thrilling rides, guests must store personal items in lockers.

Responsible Travel

Follow these tips to leave a lighter footprint, support local and have a positive impact on communities.

Theme Parks of the Future

Walt Disney World® Resort has made ecofriendly efforts across the board, from sustainable costumes and glass-recycling innovations to a 270-acre Mickey-shaped solar farm. SeaWorld Orlando has done a complete U-turn, putting much of its focus into animal conservation efforts through animal rehabilitation, visitor education and sustainably harvested foods. Even its controversial orca Shamu show is now less about whales performing tricks and more about ocean conservation.

Farm-to-Table Dining

Enjoy locally sourced, farm-fresh ingredients at **Prato** (p127) in Winter Park. Head chef Brandon McGlamery brings Italian flavors to life in new and exciting ways, all based on what's in season.

FROM LEFT: DAVIDRH/SHUTTERSTOCK ©, MATTHEW ENNIS/SHUTTERSTOCK ©

Agritourism Adventures

Agritourism has found its place in the greater Orlando area with wineries and farms galore. Enjoy a complimentary wine-tasting tour at **Lakeridge Winery & Vineyards** (p124), pick bushels of blueberries at **Tom West Blueberries** (p124) and enjoy all sorts of farm-fresh goodies – from personally picked veggies to tasty fruit preserves – at **Southern Hills Farm** (p124).

Resources

• **visitorlando.com/plan/sustainability** The sustainability page for Orlando's official travel website. • **disneyworld.disney.go.com** Walt Disney World® Resort's sustainable impact and goals. • **corporate.universaldestinationsandexperiences.com** NBCUniveral's sustainable impact and goals.

ORANGE COUNTY CONVENTION CENTER

The **Orange County Convention Center** began executing its Orange to Green sustainability campaign in 2010. Since then, it has implemented a 1mw rooftop solar PV system, used reclaimed water for landscaping and transitioned to Green Seal cleaning products.

Eco-Friendly Hotels

Across its seven properties in the greater Orlando area, Rosen Hotels & Resorts converts its used cooking oil into biodiesel; this waste-reducing fuel is then used to power their on-site maintenance vehicles and golf course equipment. The Great Lakes Orlando resort area, which includes the Ritz-Carlton Orlando and the JW Marriott Orlando, has 33 protected, undeveloped acres that are recognized as a Certified Audubon Cooperative Sanctuary. Over a dozen hotel brands in Orlando donate unused soap to Clean the World, a nonprofit that distributes recycled soap products to homeless shelters.

VOLUNTEER AT OAKLAND NATURE PRESERVE

Remove invasive plant species, help with trail maintenance or plant native seedlings. Fill out the volunteer registration form via the QR code to get the process started.

Climate Change & Travel

It's impossible to ignore the impact we have when traveling; Lonely Planet urges all travelers to engage with their travel carbon footprint, which will mainly come from air travel. While there often isn't an alternative, travelers can look to minimise the number of flights they take, opt for newer aircrafts and use cleaner ground transport, such as trains. One proposed solution – purchasing carbon offsets – unfortunately does not cancel out the impact of individual flights. While most destinations will depend on air travel for the foreseeable future, for now, pursuing ground-based travel where possible is the best course of action.

The **UN Carbon Offset Calculator** shows how flying impacts a household's emissions.

The **ICAO's carbon emissions calculator** allows visitors to analyse the CO_2 generated by point-to-point journeys.

Accessible Travel

Orlando International Airport

Orlando International Airport (MCO) works to be inclusive and accessible. This airport is recognized as an IBCCES Certified Autism Center, contains a handful of low-sensory rooms and even offers Hidden Disabilities Sunflower Lanyards to those who may need extra assistance.

Phillips Center for Performing Arts

Orlando's Dr Phillips Center of the Performing Arts (p134) is one of only four performing-arts Certified Autism Centers in the US. The venue's many sensory-friendly shows, camps and classes are run by employees specifically trained to provide accommodations for people with autism.

OUR PICK

The **Orlando Science Center** works hard to make sure that everyone feels welcome. You can request large-print daily schedules, as well as scripts for large-format films if you're hearing impaired. A limited number of wheelchairs are available for guests with mobility problems, and an American Sign Language interpreter can join you on your visit with two-weeks' notice. The Orlando Science Center has a sensory-friendly live show called *How to Feed Your Dragon*, perfect for kids 10 and under.

ACCESSIBILITY AT UNIVERSAL STUDIOS RESORT

Like Walt Disney World® Resort, Universal Orlando Resort works to make sure all guests feel welcome, regardless of disability. Scan the QR code to learn more.

Accessibility at Walt Disney World® Resort

Walt Disney World® Resort works to make sure that guests with cognitive and mobility disabilities still feel that signature Disney magic. Scan the QR code to learn more.

THE GATOR GAUNTLET

Wheelchair users can get the thrill of a lifetime at Gatorland's **Gator Gauntlet** (p124), an accessible zip line that zooms riders 350ft through the air – just don't look down!

Resources

- **visitorlando.com/plan/culture-diversity/accessibility/** The Visit Orlando tourism office provides a dedicated accessibility page that serves as a great starting point.

Nuts & Bolts

Opening Hours

Theme park opening hours change on a daily basis. Download your respective park's app for the most up-to-date information.

Banks 9am–5pm Monday–Friday, some to 1pm Saturday

Bars 4pm–midnight Monday–Thursday, noon–2am Friday–Sunday

Cafes 7am–6pm

Clubs 9pm–2am

Supermarkets 8am–9pm

Theme Parks approx 9am-10pm

Water Parks approx 10am–8pm in the warmer months (Apr–Aug) & 10am–5pm in the colder months (Sep–Mar)

QUICK INFO

Time zone Eastern Standard Time (GMT-5)

Country code +1

Emergency number 911

Population 325,000

ELECTRICITY

120V/60Hz

Public Holidays

New Year's Day January 1

Martin Luther King Jr Day January 15

Presidents' Day February

Memorial Day Late May

Independence Day July 4

Labor Day Early September

Veterans' Day November 11

Thanksgiving Late November

Christmas December 25

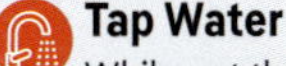

Tap Water

While not the tastiest around, tap water in Orlando is safe to drink. To neutralize the taste, consider buying a reusable water bottle with a built-in filter. Alternatively, fill up your reusable water bottle at the many designated water refill stations at popular Orlando attractions.

IFONG/SHUTTERSTOCK ©

Tickets & Opening Hours

Disney

One-day tickets Valid for admission to one Walt Disney World® park. Each park's admission price is varies.

Multiday tickets Valid for one theme park per day for each day of the ticket (you can leave/re-enter the park but cannot enter another park).

Park Hopper Gives same-day admission to any/all of the four Walt Disney World® parks. Fair warning: hopping between four parks requires a lot of stamina. Two parks a day is more feasible.

Park Hopper Plus The same as Park Hopper, but you can toss in Blizzard Beach, Typhoon Lagoon, ESPN Wide World of Sports, Oak Trail Golf Course and Walt Disney World® Resort's mini golf courses. The number of places you can visit increases the more days you buy (eg a four-day ticket allows four extra visits; a five-day ticket allows five).

TICKETS

Ticket prices for ages 10+/age 3–9.

Days	Daily Prices	Park Hopper	Park Hopper Plus
1	$119/114	$198/193	$218/213
2	$248/239	$323/324	$343/334
3	$371/357	$446/432	$466/452
4	$476/459	$561/544	$581/564
5	$517/498	$602/583	$622/603
6	$536/516	$621/601	$641/621
7	$555/534	$640/619	$660/639

OPENING HOURS

Walt Disney World® theme-park hours change by season and day to day. Generally, parks open at 8am or 9am and close sometime between 6pm and 10pm. Every day one of the four theme parks opens one hour early or closes late for guests of Walt Disney World® hotels only – these 'Magic Hours' are a major perk of staying at a Disney resort hotel.

DISNEY ©

 Genie & Lightning Lane Passes

Disney Genie is a complimentary service available in the **My Disney Experience** app. **Its My Day** feature allows you to create a park itinerary, complete with any dining bookings you may have.

With the My Disney Experience app, you'll also have the option to purchase Lightning Lane passes, allowing you to skip the regular ride lines for a fee. There are both **Lightning Lane Multi Passes** (*$15 to $40 per day*) and **Lightning Lane Single Passes** (*$10 to $28 per ride*). Each guest can purchase a maximum of two Lightning Lane Single Passes per day. Reserve early (especially the Single Passes), because they get snatched up quickly.

 Universal

Tickets for the four Universal Orlando Resort Parks start at the following prices (adult/child):

Days	One Park	Two Parks	Three Parks	Four Parks
1	$119/114 (Volcano Bay 80/75)	$174/ 169	n/a	n/a
2	n/a	$293/ 283	$349/ 339	n/a
3	n/a	$340/ 330	$375/ 365	$452/ 442
4	n/a	$360/ 350	$405/ 395	n/a

OPENING HOURS

Universal Orlando Resort theme-park hours change seasonally and daily. Generally, parks open at 8am or 9am and close sometime between 6pm and 10pm. Guests at any of the on-site hotels can enter the parks one hour before official opening times.

 Express Pass

Avoid lines at designated rides by flashing your **Express Pass** at the separate Express Pass line. These passes also give you front-section seating at select **Universal Orlando Shows** (arrive 10 to 15 minutes early to take advantage). The standard one-day pass (*theme parks/Volcano Bay $90/20*) allows one-time Express Pass access to each attraction; the unlimited version allows you unlimited access to rides (*theme parks/Volcano Bay $120/50*). Universal Orlando's deluxe resort hotels give up to five guests in each room an Unlimited Express Pass. A limited number of passes per day are available online or at the park gates. Check universalorlando.com for a calendar of prices and blackout dates. The Orlando Informer also sells Express Passes at a discounted rate (*tickets.orlandoinformer.com*).

Index

Sights p000 Map pages p000

See also separate subindexes for:
Eating p161
Drinking p162
Shopping p162

Eating

Drinking

Shopping

NOTES

Send Us Your Feedback

We love to hear from travelers – your comments help make our books better. We read every word, and we guarantee that your feedback goes straight to the authors. Visit lonelyplanet.com/contact to submit your updates and suggestions.

Note: We may edit, reproduce and incorporate your comments in Lonely Planet products such as guidebooks, websites and digital products, so let us know if you are happy to have your name acknowledged. For a copy of our privacy policy visit lonelyplanet.com/legal.

Acknowledgements

Cover photograph: Lake Eola Park. John Coletti ©

Back photograph: Orlando, Florida. VIAVAL TOURS/ Shutterstock ©

THIS BOOK

Destination Editor
Caroline Trefler

Cartographer
Julie Sheridan

Production Editor
Megan Graieg

Book Designer
Eoin Loughney

Assisting Editor
Christopher Pitts

Cover Researcher
Marc Backwell

Thanks to
Peter Cruttenden, Vicky Smith, Alison Killilea, Karen Henderson

Published by Lonely Planet Global Limited

CRN 554153

4th edition – Aug 2025

ISBN 978 1 83869 411 1

10 9 8 7 6 5 4 3 2 1

Printed in China